TEACHER'S PET PUBLICATIONS

LITPLAN TEACHER PACK
for
Our Town
based on the play by
Thornton Wilder

Written by
Mary B. Collins

© 1996 Teacher's Pet Publications
All Rights Reserved

This **LitPlan** for Thornton Wilder's
Our Town
has been brought to you by Teacher's Pet Publications, Inc.

Copyright Teacher's Pet Publications 1996
11504 Hammock Point
Berlin MD 21811

Only the student materials in this unit plan
such as worksheets, study questions, assignment sheets, and tests
may be reproduced multiple times for use in the purchaser's classroom.

For any additional copyright questions,
contact Teacher's Pet Publications.

www.tpet.com

TABLE OF CONTENTS - *Our Town*

Introduction	5
Unit Objectives	8
Reading Assignment Sheet	9
Unit Outline	10
Study Questions (Short Answer)	13
Quiz/Study Questions (Multiple Choice)	19
Pre-reading Vocabulary Worksheets	31
Lesson One (Introductory Lesson)	41
Nonfiction Assignment Sheet	43
Oral Reading Evaluation Form	53
Writing Assignment 1	51
Writing Assignment 2	54
Writing Assignment 3	63
Writing Evaluation Form	62
Vocabulary Review Activities	59
Extra Writing Assignments/Discussion ?s	57
Unit Review Activities	66
Unit Tests	69
Unit Resource Materials	97
Vocabulary Resource Materials	111

A FEW NOTES ABOUT THE AUTHOR
THORNTON WILDER

Thornton Wilder was born in Madison, Wisconsin on April 18, 1897. Because his father was appointed as American Consul General at Hong Kong and Shanghai, Mr. Wilder received his early education abroad, at a missionary school in China. Upon their return to the United States, the Wilders took up residence in California, where young Thornton Wilder attended high school at Berkeley.

Mr. Wilder entered Oberlin College in 1915 and transferred to Yale in 1917. He left college all together in 1918 to enlist in the Coast Artillery Corps but returned shortly and received his B.A. degree in 1920.

Some of his best known works are *The Bridge of San Luis Rey* (1927) which won a Pulitzer Prize, *Our Town* (1935) which won a Pulitzer Prize, *The Skin of Our Teeth* (1942) which also won a Pulitzer Prize, *The Ides of March* (1948), and *The Matchmaker* (1954) which was made into a motion picture and was used as the source for the Broadway musical *Hello, Dolly*.

INTRODUCTION

This unit has been designed to develop students' reading, writing, thinking, and language skills through exercises and activities related to *Our Town* by Thornton Wilder. It includes seventeen lessons, supported by extra resource materials.

The **introductory lesson** introduces students to one main theme of the play with a guest speaker who will speak with students about their own towns--the history, interesting people, important buildings, etc. Following the introductory activity, students are given a transition to explain how the activity relates to the play they are about to read. Following the transition, students are given the materials they will be using during the unit. At the end of the lesson, students begin the pre-reading work for the first reading assignment.

The **reading assignments** are approximately thirty pages each; some are a little shorter while others are a little longer. Students have approximately 15 minutes of pre-reading work to do prior to each reading assignment. This pre-reading work involves reviewing the study questions for the assignment and doing some vocabulary work for 8 to 10 vocabulary words they will encounter in their reading.

The **study guide questions** are fact-based questions; students can find the answers to these questions right in the text. These questions come in two formats: short answer or multiple choice. The best use of these materials is probably to use the short answer version of the questions as study guides for students (since answers will be more complete), and to use the multiple choice version for occasional quizzes. If your school has the appropriate equipment, it might be a good idea to make transparencies of your answer keys for the overhead projector.

The **vocabulary work** is intended to enrich students' vocabularies as well as to aid in the students' understanding of the play. Prior to each reading assignment, students will complete a two-part worksheet for approximately 8 to 10 vocabulary words in the upcoming reading assignment. Part I focuses on students' use of general knowledge and contextual clues by giving the sentence in which the word appears in the text. Students are then to write down what they think the words mean based on the words' usage. Part II nails down the definitions of the words by giving students dictionary definitions of the words and having students match the words to the correct definitions based on the words' contextual usage. Students should then have a good understanding of the words when they meet them in the text.

After each reading assignment, students will go back and formulate answers for the study guide questions. Discussion of these questions serves as a **review** of the most important events and ideas presented in the reading assignments.

After students complete reading the work, a lesson is devoted to the **extra discussion questions/writing assignments**. These questions focus on interpretation, critical analysis and personal response, employing a variety of thinking skills and adding to the students' understanding of the play.

Following the discussion lesson, there is a **vocabulary review** lesson which pulls together all of the fragmented vocabulary lists for the reading assignments and gives students a review of all of the words they have studied.

The **group activity** which follows the discussion questions has students working in small groups to complete a group project. Each group is responsible for making one section for a class booklet about your town.

There are three **writing assignments** in this unit, each with the purpose of informing, persuading, or having students express personal opinions. The first assignment is to inform: students write about the information they have found for the class booklet project. The second assignment is to express personal opinions: students give their opinions about what it is like to be dead. That sounds a bit morbid, but since Mr. Wilder gives his opinions throughout the play, students will be thinking about the topic in relation to the themes of the play. The third assignment is to persuade. Students persuade the teacher that life today is better than it was 100 years ago, worse than it was 100 years ago, or neither better or worse--just different from how it was 100 years ago.

In addition, there is a **nonfiction reading assignment**. Students are required to read a piece of nonfiction related in some way to *Our Town*. After reading their nonfiction pieces, students will fill out a worksheet on which they answer questions regarding facts, interpretation, criticism, and personal opinions. During one class period, students make **oral presentations** about the nonfiction pieces they have read. This not only exposes all students to a wealth of information, it also gives students the opportunity to practice **public speaking**.

The **review lesson** pulls together all of the aspects of the unit. The teacher is given four or five choices of activities or games to use which all serve the same basic function of reviewing all of the information presented in the unit.

The **unit test** comes in two formats: multiple choice or short answer. As a convenience, two different tests for each format have been included. There is also an advanced short answer unit test for more advanced students.

There are additional **support materials** included with this unit. The **extra activities** section includes suggestions for an in-class library, crossword and word search puzzles related to the play, and extra vocabulary worksheets. There is a list of **bulletin board ideas** which gives the teacher suggestions for bulletin boards to go along with this unit. In addition, there is a list of **extra class activities** the teacher could choose from to enhance the unit or as a substitution for an exercise the teacher might feel is inappropriate for his/her class. **Answer keys** are located directly after the **reproducible student materials** throughout the unit. The student materials may be reproduced for use in the teacher's classroom without infringement of copyrights. No other portion of this unit may be reproduced without the written consent of Teacher's Pet Publications, Inc.

UNIT OBJECTIVES - *Our Town*

1. Through reading Thornton Wilder's *Our Town,* students will gain a better understanding of the importance of appreciating ordinary events in our daily lives.

2. Students will demonstrate their understanding of the text on four levels: factual, interpretive, critical and personal.

3. Students will discuss the life/death theme in the play.

4. Students will be exposed to a different era of American life.

5. Students will gather information and create a booklet telling all about their town.

6. Students will be given the opportunity to practice reading aloud and silently to improve their skills in each area.

7. Students will answer questions to demonstrate their knowledge and understanding of the main events and characters in *Our Town* as they relate to the author's theme development.

8. Students will enrich their vocabularies and improve their understanding of the play through the vocabulary lessons prepared for use in conjunction with the play.

9. The writing assignments in this unit are geared to several purposes:
    a. To have students demonstrate their abilities to inform, to persuade, or to express their own personal ideas
        Note: Students will demonstrate ability to write effectively to <u>inform</u> by developing and organizing facts to convey information. Students will demonstrate the ability to write effectively to <u>persuade</u> by selecting and organizing relevant information, establishing an argumentative purpose, and by designing an appropriate strategy for an identified audience. Students will demonstrate the ability to write effectively to <u>express personal ideas</u> by selecting a form and its appropriate elements.
    b. To check the students' reading comprehension
    c. To make students think about the ideas presented by the play
    d. To encourage logical thinking
    e. To provide an opportunity to practice good grammar and improve students' use of the English language.

11. Students will read aloud, report, and participate in large and small group discussions to improve their public speaking and personal interaction skills.

READING ASSIGNMENT SHEET - *Our Town*

Date Assigned	Assignment	Completion Date
	Beginning of Act One to Mr. Webb's exit after answering Lady In A Box	
	Mr. Webb's exit to the end of Act One	
	Act Two	
	Act Three	

UNIT OUTLINE - *Our Town*

1 Guest Speaker Introduction	2 Project Assignment Parts Assignments	3 Library Project Work PV RA 1	4 Read RA 1	5 Read RA 2
6 Study ?s Act One Writing Assignment #2 PV Act Two	7 Read RA 3	8 Study ?s Act Two Practice Parts PV Act Four	9 Read RA 4	10 Study ?s Act Three Extra ?s
11 Vocabulary	12 Project Work	13 Nonfiction Reports	14 Writing Assignment #3	15 Project Conclusion
16 Review	17 **Test**			

Key: P = Preview Study Questions   V = Prereading Vocabulary Worksheets   R = Read   RA = Reading Assignment

STUDY GUIDE QUESTIONS

SHORT ANSWER STUDY GUIDE QUESTIONS - *Our Town*

Act One

1. What do you notice is different about this play as opposed to others you may be familiar with? Why do you think the author made these changes?
2. What function does the "stage manager" serve?
3. What had Doc Gibbs done early this morning?
4. What is Joe Crowell's job?
5. Who is Howie Newsome?
6. Identify George, Rebecca, Emily and Wally
7. What do Mrs. Webb and Mrs. Gibbs talk about after the children go off to school?
8. What does Mr. Webb do?
9. What does Mr. Webb say about drinking, culture and social injustice in Grover's Corners?
10. What does Emily say she'll do for George?
11. Where did Mrs. Gibbs go that evening?
12. What is Mrs. Soames' opinion of Simon Stimson?
13. What do George and Rebecca talk about just before they go to sleep?
14. What seems to be the point of the first act?

Act II

1. "You've got to love life to have life, and you've got to have life to love life." What does that mean?
2. How does this day begin as compared to the day in the first act?
3. What event is taking place this day?
4. What is Mrs. Gibbs worried about?
5. "Everybody has a right to their own troubles." Explain.
6. Why couldn't Mrs. Webb invite George into her home on his wedding day?
7. What advice does Mr. Webb give to George?
8. How did George and Emily decide that they were "meant for each other"?
9. What "typical" things happened at the wedding?
10. What was the "topic" of Act II?

Our Town Short Answer Study Guide Page 2

Act III
1. How many years have passed since Act II?
2. What is the setting of Act III?
3. Which of the characters we have met in Act I and Act II are now in the cemetery, and how did they die?
4. How does the stage manager describe death?
5. Identify Sam Craig. What is his function as a character?
6. How did Emily die?
7. How does Emily describe the living?
8. Emily says, "I never realized before how troubled and how . . . how in the dark live persons are." Explain.
9. Mrs. Gibbs says, "Choose the least important day of your life. It will be important enough." What does she mean?
10. How did the day of Emily's twelfth birthday begin, compared to the days in Act I and Act II? What is the significance of that?
11. "Oh, earth, you're too wonderful for anybody to realize you!" Explain what Emily is expressing here.
12. "Mother Gibbs," said Emily, ". . . They don't understand, do they?" What don't they understand, and who are "they"?

ANSWER KEY: SHORT ANSWER STUDY GUIDE QUESTIONS - *Our Town*

Act One

1. What do you notice is different about this play as opposed to others you may be familiar with? Why do you think the author made these changes?
    The most obvious differences are the lack of much scenery or many props and the role of the stage manager as one who talks to the audience. We'll also see, as we progress, the lack of a real "plot" since the play is one simply describing ordinary life.

2. What function does the "stage manager" serve?
    The stage manager functions to give the audience background information and present Mr. Wilder's views on many issues. Also, he helps to bring the audience into the play, making it easier for them to identify Our Town with their own town.

3. What had Doc Gibbs done early this morning?
    He had just delivered twins over in the "Polish section of town." This is symbolically significant as the play opens to show "birth" in the first act, later followed by life, marriage, and death.

4. What is Joe Crowell's job?
    Joe delivers newspapers.

5. Who is Howie Newsome?
    Howie is the milkman.

6. Identify George, Rebecca, Emily and Wally
    George and Rebecca are the Gibbs' children; Emily and Wally are the Webbs' children.

7. What do Mrs. Webb and Mrs. Gibbs talk about after the children go off to school?
    They have an ordinary conversation about the weather and what each family is doing. The most important part of their conversation is about Mrs. Gibbs' being offered $350 for a piece of her furniture. This will come up again later at the end of the play when we find out that she did in fact sell the furniture and get the money, never went to Europe, and willed the money to Emily and George.

8. What does Mr. Webb do?
    Mr. Webb is the editor of the local newspaper.

9. What does Mr. Webb say about drinking, culture and social injustice in Grover's Corners?
    They have a few town drunks, like any town does. They have little in the way of cultural activities. They are just as concerned as everyone else is about social injustice, but, like everyone else, they haven't found a solution yet.

10. What does Emily say she'll do for George?
    She will help him study -- give him "hints" about schoolwork problems.

11. Where did Mrs. Gibbs go that evening?
    Mrs. Gibbs went to choir practice.

12. What is Mrs. Soames' opinion of Simon Stimson?
    She thinks that his drinking problem is the worst scandal in the town.

13. What do George and Rebecca talk about just before they go to sleep?
    They talk about the moon. Rebecca thinks it is getting closer; George tells her that if it were, someone would tell them. Then, Rebecca tells George about a letter with a strangely written address.

14. What seems to be the point of the first act?
    The point is to introduce the characters and show them in their daily lives doing nothing special, just living in an ordinary day.

Act II
1. "You've got to love life to have life, and you've got to have life to love life." What does that mean?
    You have to appreciate life to make your life fuller; when you don't have life anymore, you can't appreciate life as you could have when you were alive.

2. How does this day begin as compared to the day in the first act?
    It starts out almost exactly the same, with the exception that Si Crowell is delivering papers now instead of his brother, and Howie has to leave extra milk for the wedding guests for Mrs. Webb and Mrs. Gibbs. The point is, though, that things don't change much in Grover's Corners; the newspaper boy still delivers papers, the milkman still comes, every day starts out pretty much the same.

3. What event is taking place this day?
    George and Emily are getting married.

4. What is Mrs. Gibbs worried about?
    Mrs. Gibbs is worried that Emily won't take care of George as well as she (Mrs. Gibbs) has (something just about every mother worries about on her son's wedding day).

5. "Everybody has a right to their own troubles." Explain.
    Dr. and Mrs. Gibbs have to mind their own business and let the children live their own lives. Right or wrong, full of mistakes or not, people have the right to make their own decisions and a right to work through their lives as they see fit. In a sense, troubles could be seen in the context of this play as some of those little things people don't appreciate.

Without troubles contrasting to the good times, life would be dull. Also, in the context of the play, thank heavens we do have the right to work out our own troubles without interference or advice by unwanted parties.

6. Why couldn't Mrs. Webb invite George into her home on his wedding day?
    There is a superstition that the bride and groom can't see each other before the wedding ceremony, or they will have bad luck.

7. What advice does Mr. Webb give to George?
    Mr. Webb tells George to ignore most advice which will be given to him.

8. How did George and Emily decide that they were "meant for each other"?
    They had been admiring each other from afar for some time, and Emily had been helping George with his schoolwork earlier. What really brought out the relationship, though, was Emily's comment to George about his character. George realized that if Emily thought enough of him to bring a flaw in his character to his attention, she must really care for him. He, then, could tell her that he cared for her, too. This all came out in a conversation at the local soda fountain.

9. What "typical" things happened at the wedding?
    The bride and groom got cold feet, expressed their second-thoughts about getting married. The ladies cried and remarked on what a beautiful wedding it was.

10. What was the "topic" of Act II?
    Love and marriage was the topic of Act II.

Act III
1. How many years have passed since Act II?
    Nine years have passed.

2. What is the setting of Act III?
    Act III is set in the cemetery, except for Emily's twelfth birthday.

3. Which of the characters we have met in Act I and Act II are now buried in the cemetery, and how did they die?
    Mrs. Gibbs died of pneumonia. Mr. Stimson hanged himself. Wally Webb's appendix burst. Mrs. Soames is also in the cemetery, but the text gives no reason.

4. How does the stage manager describe death?
    He says that dead people get "weaned away from earth." They gradually lose interest in the things they had and people they loved.

5. Identify Sam Craig. What is his function as a character?
   Sam is Mrs. Gibbs' nephew. He has been out of town and needs to be filled in on what has happened to many townspeople. As he is given background information, so is the audience.

6. How did Emily die?
   Emily died in childbirth.

7. How does Emily describe the living?
   She says "they're sort-of shut-up in little boxes."

8. Emily says, "I never realized before how troubled and how . . . how in the dark live persons are." Explain.
   People get so busy with their own thoughts, ambitions and problems that they don't take time to open themselves up to try to see, understand and appreciate everything in the world.

9. Mrs. Gibbs says, "Choose the least important day of your life. It will be important enough." What does she mean?
   Even the least important days of our lives are full of things we should appreciate and would miss if they were gone. Every day is special because we are alive to enjoy it.

10. How did the day of Emily's twelfth birthday begin, compared to the days in Act I and Act II? What is the significance of that?
    It began just the same as the other days. Again, the point is that all days in Grover's Corners start out about the same. Most days in most peoples' lives are repetitious in nature. There is a routine that is carried out, certain things that are always done. That doesn't make them less important, but it does make it easier for people to take those things for granted.

11. "Oh, earth, you're too wonderful for anybody to realize you!" Explain what Emily is expressing here.
    There are so many things to appreciate, so many things to be thankful for and enjoy that it is impossible for any one person to grasp the importance or greatness of everything in the world.

12. "Mother Gibbs," said Emily, ". . . They don't understand, do they?" What don't they understand, and who are "they"?
    "They" are living people. They don't understand the importance of enjoying every moment of life.

MULTIPLE CHOICE STUDY GUIDE/QUIZ QUESTIONS - *Our Town*

<u>Act One</u>

1. True or False: This play differs from most others in that there is a lack of scenery and the role of the stage manager is one who talks to the audience. There is also the lack of a real "plot."
    a. True
    b. False

2. The stage manager serves many functions. Which of these is not one of them?
    a. Giving the audience background information.
    b. Presenting the author's view on many issues.
    c. Making sure the audience can see and hear the actors.
    d. Bringing the audience into the play, making it easier for them to identify the setting with their own town.

3. What had Doc Gibbs done early this morning?
    a. He had performed an appendectomy on the town's mayor.
    b. He had delivered twins over in the "Polish section of town."
    c. He had helped one of the local farmers put some sick cattle out of their misery.
    d. He had overslept and missed his first three appointments.

4. What is Joe Crowell's job?
    a. He is the owner of the town's busiest restaurant.
    b. He is the sheriff.
    c. He is a bank clerk.
    d. He delivers newspapers.

5. Who is Howie Newsome?
    a. He is the veterinarian.
    b. He is Doc Gibb's ne'er-do-well cousin who is there visiting.
    c. He is the milkman.
    d. He is a traveling insurance salesman who comes by every three months.

6. True or False: George and Emily are the Webb's children. Rebecca and Wally are the Gibbs' children.
    a. True
    b. False

Our Town Multiple Choice Study Questions Page 2

7. True or False: After the children go off to school, Mrs. Webb and Mrs. Gibbs have an ordinary conversation. The most important part of it is when Mrs. Gibbs tells Mrs. Webb she is thinking about selling a piece of furniture for $350.00.
    a. True
    b. False

8. What does Mr. Webb do?
    a. He is the mayor.
    b. He is the owner of the grocery store.
    c. He is the editor of the newspaper.
    d. He is the school principal

9. True or False: These are Mr. Webb's comments about drinking, culture and social injustice in Grover's Corners: They have fewer drunks than other towns; they have an abundance of cultural activities; they have erased social injustice in their every day lives.
    a. True
    b. False

10. What does Emily say she'll do for George?
    a. She'll teach him to dance before the prom.
    b. She'll introduce him to her girlfriend, Whom George has been wanting to meet.
    c. She'll bake him a chocolate cake every week for a month.
    d. She'll help him study--give him hints about schoolwork problems.

11. Where did Mrs. Gibbs go that evening?
    a. She went to choir practice.
    b. She went to play bridge.
    c. She went to her class at the college.
    d. She went shopping with a friend.

12. What is Mrs. Soames's opinion of Simon Stimson?
    a. She feels sorry for him.
    b. She thinks his drinking problem is the worst scandal in the town.
    c. She thinks the church should have a program to help people like him.
    d. She thinks his problem is symbolic of the impending doom of the world.

13. True or False: Before George and Rebecca go to sleep, they talk about the moon. Rebecca thinks it is getting closer: George tells her that if it were, someone would tell them, then Rebecca tells George about a letter with a strangely written address.
    a. True
    b. False

Our Town Multiple Choice Study Questions Page 3

14. What seems to be the point of the first act?
    a. The point is to foreshadow the action of the later acts.
    b. The point is to show the contrast between appearance and reality in their lives.
    c. The point is to introduce the characters and show them in their ordinary daily lives.
    d. The point is to build suspense for the dramatic conclusion to come.

Our Town Multiple Choice Study Questions Page 4

Act II

15. Which of these lines from the play can be interpreted to mean that one has to appreciate life to make life fuller; when one doesn't have life anymore, one can't appreciate life as one could have when alive?
    a. "There isn't much culture, but maybe this is the place to tell you that we've got a lot of pleasures of a kind here; we like the sun comin' up over the mountain in the morning, and we notice a good deal about the birds."
    b. "You've got to love life to have life, and you've got to have life to love life.
    c. We're all hunting like everybody else for a way the diligent and sensible can rise to the top and the lazy and quarrelsome can sink to the bottom.
    d. Now there are some things we all know, but we don't take'm out and look at'm very often. We all know that something is eternal...and that something has to do with human beings.

16. The second day begins almost the same as the first act, with the exception that Si Crowell is delivering papers now instead of his brother, and Howie has to leave extra milk for the wedding guests. What is the point of this?
    a. Things don't change much in Grover's Corners; every day starts out pretty much the same.
    b. Life is in a constant state of flux and turmoil, as represented in the microcosm of Grover's Corners.
    c. It shows that Si and Howie are the ones in the play who will be different than the other characters; they will be going against society, one of the main conflicts in the play.
    d. It doesn't mean anything. It's just a part of the story.

17. What event is taking place this day?
    a. George and Emily are getting married.
    b. Si Crowell is coming home from the war with a purple heart.
    c. The city is going to become fully hooked up with electricity.
    d. The new school building is going to be dedicated.

18. What is Mrs. Gibbs worried about?
    a. She is worried that she is getting old and may lapse into poor health.
    b. She is worried that the heat is going to spoil the day's festivities.
    c. She is worried that her son is not going to be properly cared for once she is not doing the caretaking.
    d. She is neurotic, and worries about everything.

Our Town Multiple Choice Study Questions Page 5

19. "Everybody has a right to their own troubles." How are troubles seen in the play?
    a. They are seen as a great burden.
    b. They are seen as some of those little things people don't appreciate; as a contrast to the good times.
    c. They are seen as the backbone of character building.
    d. They are seen as folly caused by people's own humanity.

20. Why couldn't Mrs. Webb invite George into her home on his wedding day?
    a. He was getting married in the "wrong" church, and she had to show her disapproval.
    b. Mr. Gibbs was angry because they had not been invited to the wedding. He had forbidden her to talk to George.
    c. She was embarrassed to have the house looking less than perfect for guests.
    d. There was a superstition that the bride and groom could not see each other before the wedding ceremony, or they would have bad luck.

21. What advice does Mr. Webb give to George?
    a. To stop drinking and smoking while he is still young, so that he doesn't ruin his health.
    b. To buy when the market is low, and sell when it is high.
    c. To ignore most of the advice which will be given to him.
    d. To trust in the Lord to lead him on the right path.

22. George and Emily decided that they were "meant for each other" for several reasons. Which of the following is not one of the reasons?
    a. They had been admiring each other from afar for some time.
    b. They were born on the same day in the same year, were the same height, and had the same general average in high school.
    c. Emily had been helping George with his schoolwork earlier.
    d. George realized that if Emily thought enough of him to bring a flaw in his character to his attention, that she must really care for him.

23. Many "typical" things happened at the wedding. Which of these was not one of them?
    a. The bride and groom smashed cake in each other's faces.
    b. The bridge and groom got cold feet.
    c. The father gave away the bride.
    d. The ladies cried.

24. What was the "topic" of Act II?
    a. It was birth and death.
    b. It was the sameness of life.
    c. It was love and marriage.
    d. It was the importance of children.

Our Town Multiple Choice Study Questions Page 6

Act III

25. How many years have passed since Act II?
    a. Twenty-five years have passed.
    b. Only one year has passed.
    c. Sixteen years have passed.
    d. Nine years have passed.

26. What is the setting of Act III?
    a. It is set in the schoolhouse.
    b. It is set in the cemetery.
    c. It is set in the Gibb's living room.
    d. It is set in the park.

27. Some of the characters we have met previously are now dead. Which of the following is not dead?
    a. Mrs. Gibbs
    b. Professor Willard
    c. Mrs. Soames
    d. Mr. Stimson

28. How does the stage manager describe death?
    a. He says that dead people get "weaned away from earth." They gradually lose interest in the things they had and the people they loved.
    b. He says that most people leave the world kicking and screaming, just the way they come into it.
    c. He says that death is a highly personal experience, and can't really be accurately described except by the person who is dying, so we will never really know what it is like.
    d. He is very matter-of-fact, and says it is just a part of life.

29. A new character, Sam Craig, has been introduced. What is his function?
    a. The author is setting the play up so that we can write a sequel if this first one is well-received by the audience.
    b. It is a symbolism that things change.
    c. While the character is being filled in on background information, so is the audience.
    d. His function is to bring Grover's Corners into the modern world.

Our Town Multiple Choice Study Questions Page 7

30. How did Emily die?
    a. She contracted a rare disease. The doctor in town didn't know what it was, and by the time he sent her to a specialist in the city, she was too ill to be helped.
    b. She committed suicide by drowning.
    c. She was run over by a drunk driver.
    d. She died in childbirth.

31. Emily says, "they're sort of shut up in little boxes." Whom is she describing?
    a. She is describing the living.
    b. She is describing the dead.
    c. She is describing her brother's pet bugs.
    d. She is joking about how birthday and wedding presents must feel inside their boxes. In the play, the little boxes are symbols of people's small minds and petty problems.

32. Emily says, "I never realized before how troubled and how . . . how in the dark live persons are." What does she mean?
    a. Now that she is in heaven, she is happy and her troubles are over.
    b. She was in a state of denial when she was alive, and thought everyone else was perfect.
    c. People get so busy with their own thoughts, ambitions and problems that they don't take time to open themselves up to try and see, understand, and appreciate everything in the world.
    d. Death brings insight that life couldn't possibly give.

33. True or False: Mrs. Gibbs thinks even the least important days of our lives are full of things we should appreciate and would miss if they were gone.
    a. True
    b. False

34. What is the significance of the way the day of Emily's twelfth birthday began?
    a. It showed that most people's lives are repetitious in nature.
    b. It foreshadowed her death.
    c. It emphasized that the climax of the play was in Act Three.
    d. It served as a catharsis for the audience.

35. What did Emily say about life?
    a. "Ignorance and blindness are all there really is."
    b. "The strain's so bad that every sixteen hours everybody lies down and gets a rest."
    c. "Oh, earth, you're too wonderful for anybody to realize you!"
    d. "There are some surprises waiting for you on the table.

Our Town Multiple Choice Study Questions Page 8

36. "Mother Gibbs," said Emily, ". . . They don't understand, do they?" What don't they understand, and who are "they"?
    a. They are the audience, and they don't understand the true meaning of the play.
    b. They are the poor souls who died without the salvation of religion.
    c. They are the living who don't understand the importance of enjoying every moment of life.
    d. They are the relatives of the deceased. They don't understand how happy the dead are to be free of the burden of life.

ANSWER KEY - MULTIPLE CHOICE STUDY/QUIZ QUESTIONS
Our Town

Act One		Act Two		Act Three	
1.	A	15.	B	25.	D
2.	C	16.	A	26.	B
3.	B	17.	A	27.	B
4.	D	18.	C	28.	A
5.	C	19.	B	29.	C
6.	B	20.	D	30.	D
7.	A	21.	C	31.	A
8.	C	22.	B	32.	C
9.	B	23.	A	33.	A
10.	D	24.	C	34.	A
11.	A			35.	C
12.	B			36.	C
13.	A				
14.	C				

PREREADING VOCABULARY WORKSHEETS

VOCABULARY - *Our Town*

Reading Assignment 1
Part I: Using Prior Knowledge and Contextual Clues
    Below are the sentences in which the vocabulary words appear in the text. Read the sentence. Use any clues you can find in the sentence combined with your prior knowledge, and write what you think the underlined words mean in the space provided.

1. Two arched <u>trellises</u>, covered with vines and flowers, are pushed out, one by each <u>proscenium</u> pillar

2. This is Mrs. Gibbs' garden. Corn ... peas ... beans ... hollyhocks ... heliotrope ... and a lot of <u>burdock</u>.

3. Strawberry <u>phosphates</u>--that's what you spend it on.

4. Well, I did beat about the bush a little and said that if I got a <u>legacy</u>--that's the way I put it-- I'd make him take me somewhere.

5. Is there no one in town aware of social <u>injustice</u> and industrial inequality?

6. I guess we're all hunting like everybody else for a way the <u>diligent</u> and sensible can rise to the top and the lazy and quarrelsome can sink to the bottom.

Part II: Determining the Meaning
    Match the words to their dictionary definitions.

___ 1. trellises   A. violation of another's rights or of what is right
___ 2. proscenium   B. marked by persevering, painstaking effort
___ 3. burdock   C. a soda fountain drink with carbonated water and flavored syrup
___ 4. phosphates   D. prickly, weed-like plant with purple flower
___ 5. legacy   E. structures used for supporting vines and creeping plants
___ 6. injustice   F. something handed down from an ancestor
___ 7. diligent   G. stage area between curtain and orchestra

Reading Assignment 2 Vocabulary *Our Town*

Part I: Using Prior Knowledge and Contextual Clues
Below are the sentences in which the vocabulary words appear in the text. Read the sentence. Use any clues you can find in the sentence combined with your prior knowledge, and write what you think the underlined words mean in the space provided.

1. . . . some scientific fellas have found a way of painting all this reading matter with a glue--a silicate glue--that'll make it keep a thousand--two thousand years.

2. . . . --this is the way we were in the provinces north of New York at the beginning of the twentieth century.

3. Naturally, I didn't want to say a word about it in front of those others, but now we're alone-- really, it's the worst scandal that ever was in this town.

4. I can see Mr. Soames scowling at the window now. You'd think we'd been to a dance the way the menfolk carry on.

5. Come out and smell the heliotrope in the moonlight.

6. What were the girls gossiping about tonight?

7. They haven't got nothing fit to burgle and everybody knows it.

Part II: Determining the Meaning
Match the words to their dictionary definitions.

___ 8. silicate   A. flowers native to Peru, having fragrant, purple flowers
___ 9. provinces   B. spreading rumors or talk of a personal or sensational nature
___ 10. scandal   C. steal
___ 11. scowling   D. compound containing silicone, oxygen and one or more metals
___ 12. heliotrope   E. frowning in anger or disapproval
___ 13. gossiping   F. areas situated away from the population center
___ 14. burgle   G. an incident that brings about disgrace or offends society

Reading Assignment 3 Vocabulary *Our Town*

Part I: Using Prior Knowledge and Contextual Clues
   Below are the sentences in which the vocabulary words appear in the text. Read the sentence. Use any clues you can find in the sentence combined with your prior knowledge, and write what you think the underlined words mean in the space provided.

1. Nature's been pushing and <u>contriving</u> in other ways, too: a number of young people fell in love and got married.

2. Mrs. Gibbs: At the table, drinking her coffee <u>meditatively</u>.

3. Well, you and I been conversing for twenty years now without any noticeable <u>barren</u> spells.

4. George crosses the stage to his own home, bewildered and <u>crestfallen</u>. He slowly dodges a puddle and disappears into his house.

5. . . . and you never stopped to speak to anybody any more. Not even to your own family you didn't . . . and, George, it's a fact you've got awful <u>conceited</u> and stuck-up . . . .

6. Stage Manager: Pretending to be <u>affronted</u>

7. In half-amused <u>exasperation</u>.

8. The stage is suddenly arrested into silent <u>tableau</u>.

Reading Assignment 3 Vocabulary *Our Town* Continued

Part II: Determining the Meaning
　　Match the vocabulary words to their definitions.

___15. contriving	A. as if deeply pondering a point
___16. meditatively	B. empty; bare
___17. barren	C. vain; holding an unusually high opinion of oneself
___18. crestfallen	D. feeling of impatient anger or annoyance
___19. conceited	E. planning with cleverness or ingenuity
___20. affronted	F. an interlude during a scene when all performers freeze momentarily
___21. exasperation	G. dejected; dispirited or depressed
___22. tableau	H. intentionally insulted

Reading Assignment 4 Vocabulary *Our Town*

Part I: Using Prior Knowledge and Contextual Clues
　　Below are the sentences in which the vocabulary words appear in the text. Read the sentence. Use any clues you can find in the sentence combined with your prior knowledge, and write what you think the underlined words mean in the space provided.

1. When they speak their tone is matter-of-fact, without sentimentality and, above all, without lugubriousness.

2. We all know that *something* is eternal.

3. They get weaned away from earth--that's the way I put it,--weaned away.

4. And they stay here while the earth part of 'em burns away, burns out; and all that time they slowly get indifferent to what's goin' on in Grover's Corners.

5. Mostly the bereaved pick a verse.

6. She throws an anguished glance at the stage manager.

7. She looks toward the stage manager and asks abruptly through her tears . . . .

8. With mounting violence; bitingly

Reading Assignment 4 Vocabulary *Our Town* Continued

Part II: Determining the Meaning
    Match the vocabulary words to their dictionary definitions.

___23. lugubriousness   A. slowly detached from something it is used to having
___24. eternal   B. in a short or brusque manner
___25. weaned   C. agonized; tormented
___26. indifferent   D. lasting forever
___27. bereaved   E. in a nasty way intending to hurt someone
___28. anguished   F. gloominess; ridiculously dismal
___29. abruptly   G. having no particular interest or concern for
___30. bitingly   H. suffering the loss of a loved one

ANSWER KEY - VOCABULARY
Our Town

Reading Assignment 1
1. E
2. G
3. D
4. C
5. F
6. A
7. B

Reading Assignment 2
8. D
9. F
10. G
11. E
12. A
13. B
14. C

Reading Assignment 3
15. E
16. A
17. B
18. G
19. C
20. H
21. D
22. F

Reading Assignment 4
23. F
24. D
25. A
26. G
27. H
28. C
29. B
30. E

DAILY LESSONS

LESSON ONE

Objectives
    1. To introduce the *Our Town* unit.
    2. To distribute books and other related materials

NOTE: Prior to this lesson, you need to contact a guest speaker and make the necessary arrangements. Call your local newspaper office and try to arrange for the most experienced reporter of news and events in your area to come talk with your class about your town. Most newspaper offices have someone who has been reporting about the local area for decades. If a reporter isn't available, or if you prefer, you could find someone or several people who have lived in your area for many years to come talk with your students about things that have happened in your town and changes that have been made over the years. If there are no willing or able reporters and no senior citizens who want to come to your class, try getting someone from your local historical society.

    It might be a good idea, too, to have each student write down three questions to ask your guest speaker in case your speaker doesn't come with a presentation planned. Sometimes it is good to have some planned questions to start things off, to get a discussion going or to help your speaker feel comfortable and get him/her on track.

Activity #1
    Introduce your guest speaker. If your speaker has not come with a presentation planned, have students ask their questions to get a discussion going. Perhaps your speaker could bring some pictures of the way town "used to look." Spend most of your class time with the guest speaker talking about the way town used to be, things that have happened in your town through the years, general "I remember when . . ." kinds of things. If your students and speaker are enjoying each other, let the discussion go all period.

Activity #2
    If you don't have time for this activity, do it in Lesson Two.

Distribute the materials students will use in this unit. Explain in detail how students are to use these materials.

    Study Guides Students should read the study guide questions for each reading assignment prior to beginning the reading assignment to get a feeling for what events and ideas are important in the section they are about to read. After reading the section, students will (as a class or individually) answer the questions to review the important events and ideas from that section of the play. Students should keep the study guides as study materials for the unit test.

Vocabulary   Prior to reading a reading assignment, students will do vocabulary work related to the section of the play they are about to read. Following the completion of the reading of the play, there will be a vocabulary review of all the words used in the vocabulary assignments. Students should keep their vocabulary work as study materials for the unit test.

Reading Assignment Sheet   You need to fill in the reading assignment sheet to let students know by when their reading has to be completed. You can either write the assignment sheet up on a side blackboard or bulletinboard and leave it there for students to see each day, or you can "ditto" copies for each student to have. In either case, you should advise students to become very familiar with the reading assignments so they know what is expected of them.

Extra Activities Center   The Extra Activities portion of this unit contains suggestions for an extra library of related books and articles in your classroom as well as crossword and word search puzzles. Make an extra activities center in your room where you will keep these materials for students to use. (Bring the books and articles in from the library and keep several copies of the puzzles on hand.) Explain to students that these materials are available for students to use when they finish reading assignments or other class work early.

Nonfiction Assignment Sheet   Explain to students that they each are to read at least one non-fiction piece from the in-class library at some time during the unit. Students will fill out a nonfiction assignment sheet after completing the reading to help you evaluate their reading experiences and to help the students think about and evaluate their own reading experiences.

Books   Each school has its own rules and regulations regarding student use of school books. Advise students of the procedures that are normal for your school.

NONFICTION ASSIGNMENT SHEET
(To be completed after reading the required nonfiction article)

Name _____ Date _____

Title of Nonfiction Read _____

Written By _____ Publication Date _____

I. Factual Summary: Write a short summary of the piece you read.

II. Vocabulary
    1. With which vocabulary words in the piece did you encounter some degree of difficulty?

    2. How did you resolve your lack of understanding with these words?

III. Interpretation: What was the main point the author wanted you to get from reading his work?

IV. Criticism
    1. With which points of the piece did you agree or find easy to accept? Why?

    2. With which points of the piece did you disagree or find difficult to believe? Why?

V. Personal Response: What do you think about this piece? OR How does this piece influence your ideas?

LESSON TWO

Objectives
1. To make students aware of the things their own towns have to offer
2. To give students experience doing research in and out of the library
3. To give students the opportunity to practice writing to inform
4. To create a booklet about your town
5. To give the teacher the opportunity to evaluate students' writing skills
6. To assign speaking parts for Act One

Activity #1

Assign students parts to read orally for *Our Town*. Explain to students that in Lesson Four (give students a day/date) they will be reading their parts orally and will be graded on their reading. Suggest that it would be a good idea to look over their lines and practice them between now and then.

Activity #2

Divide your class into eight groups. Distribute the Project Assignment sheet and Writing Assignment #1. Discuss the directions in detail, and give students the remainder of the class period to work.

LESSON THREE

Objectives
1. To give students the chance to get started on their projects
2. To make the library resources available to students who may need them for their projects
3. To preview the study questions for Act One
4. To do the prereading vocabulary work for Act One

Activity #1

Take students to the library. Tell them that they have this class period to work on their project assignments, that they are in the library for those students who need the library's resources for their research. (Many school libraries have phone books and telephones. The phone book is one good source of information, and if it is not against school policies, perhaps some students could use the library's phone to call various places for the information they need.)

Activity #2

Tell all students that they should preview the study questions and do the prereading vocabulary work for Act One prior to your next class period. If some students do not need the library resources for their projects and have no more in class work they can do on their projects, they could begin the prereading work for Act One.

SPEAKING PART ASSIGNMENTS - *Our Town*

Reading Assignment 1/Act One
Stage Manager
Dr. Gibbs
Joe Crowell, Jr.
Howie Newsome
Mrs. Gibbs
Mrs. Webb
Rebecca
Wally
George
Prof. Willard
Belligerent Man
Lady In A Box
Woman In The Balcony

Reading Assignment 3/Act Two
Stage Manager
Howie Newsome
Si Crowell
Constable Warren
Mrs. Gibbs
Mrs. Webb
Dr. Gibbs
George
Mr. Webb
Emily
Baseball Players
Mrs. Soames

Reading Assignment 2/Act One
Stage Manager
Emily
Mr. Webb
George
Mrs. Webb
Simon Stimson
Dr. Gibbs
Mrs. Gibbs
Mrs. Soames
Rebecca
Constable Warren

Reading Assignment 4/Act Three
Stage Manager
Sam Craig
Joe Stoddard
Mrs. Gibbs
Simon Stimson
Mrs. Soames
Woman Among The Dead
Mr. Webb
Joe Crowell
Constable Warren
Mr. Carter
Emily
Man Among The Dead

PROJECT ASSIGNMENT - *Our Town*

PROMPT

The play you are going to read is about the people who live in a little town called Grover's Corners. Grover's Corners is just an average little town where ordinary people live out their ordinary lives. Folks who live there might even call it a boring little place. Even places that seem boring or ordinary to us have special things, as we will see in the case of Grover's Corners.

It's easy to get bored with things, to just get into a rut, a routine, and let the world pass by. Sometimes we just stop noticing things. Have you ever noticed something has changed and then you found out that it had been changed days, weeks, or even months ago--that you just hadn't noticed it? Perhaps you walk or ride past the same buildings every day on the way to school. What do you really know about the buildings and places in your town? Are they just *there*, or do you really know about them? For that matter, what do you really know about the town or city where you live? Is it just *there*, a place where you carry out your daily routine, or do you really know about and understand what's going on in your town?

Your assignment is, as a class, to create a booklet about your own town.

HOW?

Each of you has been assigned to a group. Each of your groups has been (or will now be) assigned to one of the following topics:
- Town History
- Important People--Past and Present
- Landmarks/Historical or Important Buildings
- Economy/Jobs/Businesses/Industries
- Restaurant Guide
- Statistics
- Things To Do
- Community Organizations/Clubs

Each of your groups will be responsible for creating one section of the booklet. You will have planning time and some time to do any necessary research. Then each group will produce its section of the book. After all the sections are completed, we'll get back together as a class to look at each section and to put the booklet together.

REQUIREMENTS

1. Each group member must have specific tasks for which he/she is responsible.
2. A Project Worksheet must be completed for each group and handed in with the group's booklet section.
3. The groups' booklet sections must be typed (or printed out from a computer) on 8-1/2" X 11" paper.
4. Each group must submit at least 3 photographs (black and white) to go along with its booklet section. (Photos may be taken by you with a camera, clipped from a newspaper, or taken from a photo album or photo file.)

Our Town Project Assignment   Page 2

      5. The information in your booklet section must be accurate and thorough.
      6. Writing Assignment #1 is also a part of this project. You must complete it and hand it in with your booklet sections.
      7. Each group must submit a proposed cover for the finished booklet.
      8. Each group must prepare enough copies of its section for each member of the class.

GETTING STARTED

History Group - Find out when your town was founded. Figure out how many years ago that was. Divide the number of years by the number of people in your group. Assign each student in your group that many years of your town's history to cover. For example, if your town was founded 125 years ago and there are 5 members in your group, each member should have to cover roughly 25 years of your town's history. Student 1 would cover from the founding date (FD) to FD + 25 years. Student 2 would cover from FD+25years to FD+50 years. Student 3 would cover FD+50 years to FD+75 years, and so on.

Important People Group - Brainstorm a list of important people from the past and present in your town. You may use a person's position if you do not yet know his/her name. For example, you could say "mayors" meaning you want to find out and report on the people who have been your town's mayors through the years. You can brainstorm a general list in this way, and then you will need to go do some research to find specific people's names so you can research individuals. Some ideas are: the people who founded your town, your mayors and other government officials, community and business leaders, famous people who were born in your town (actors, sports figures, military personnel, etc.), and so on. Be on the lookout for pictures of these people. Check your local newspaper (past and present issues), interview lots of people asking them for a list of the ten most important people in your town (or in your town's history), or check in your library for information about the people in your town. After you have made a list of specific names, assign each group member different people to research.

Things To Do Group - Brainstorm a list of categories of things to do. (Amusement parks, museums, state or federal parks, theaters, movies, special events, etc. -- anything that falls under the category of "Things To Do" can be included.) You may need to research to find out all the things your town has to offer; there may be things to do that you haven't heard about. Check your local newspaper and the phone book. The chamber of commerce also may have information that would be helpful. After you have a complete list of things to do, assign each group member different places/things to research.

Our Town Project Assignment   Page 3

Landmarks Group - What buildings, monuments, or landmarks are in your town? Make a list of all the important buildings (courthouse, home of the person who founded your town, headquarters of major corporations, etc.), monuments, or landmarks (rivers, "named" trees, mountains, etc.) that are in your area. This may require some research. You might check with your local chamber of commerce or your local library. After you have compiled a list, assign each group member specific landmarks to research in detail.

Economy - What jobs, businesses, or industries are in your town? What kind of work do people in your town do? Make a complete list of jobs, businesses and industries that are important to your town. This may require some research. There may be reports published about the economics in your town. If so, they would probably be on file at your courthouse, town hall, or public library. The chamber of commerce is also a good source of information. When you have a complete list, assign each group member specific businesses/industries/jobs to research in detail.

Community Organizations & Clubs - What clubs and organizations are in your town? Who are they, who belongs to them (you don't have to get complete membership lists!), and what do they contribute to your town? Make a list of the clubs and organizations. This may require some research. Check your phone book, newspaper, and town hall for information. When you have compiled a list, assign each group member specific organizations and clubs to research in detail.

Restaurant Guide Group - Make a list of the restaurants and carry-out places in your town. The phone book is a good place to start for information. Assign each member of your group a kind of restaurant to research (Chinese foods, Mexican foods, Steak pubs, fast foods, etc.). Each group member should make a list of the specific restaurants in his/her category, find out what's on the menu, what house specialties are, what the price range is for lunch or dinner, any awards or ratings the restaurant has, etc.)

Statistics Group - You are the catch-all group for miscellaneous information. The kind of information you will be gathering might all begin, "Did you know that . . . ." because you're to find interesting facts and tidbits of information about your town. Brainstorm a list of ideas you have for kinds of information you think you might find. For example, things like population, birth and death rates, average annual income, how much it costs to run your school system, how much your town spends on roads or snow removal, etc. Each group member should be assigned to find 10 interesting facts about your town. You will get back together and decide which of the tidbits of information will be published in your section of the booklet.

<u>IN ADDITION</u>

Each person in the group has specific information to research. In addition, each group member must have at least one task relating to the production of your section of the booklet. For example, one student may type and print your section, one student may proofread, one student may be your "fact-getter" when questions arise, one student may be your "go-for" person who

Our Town Project Assignment   Page 4

goes and gets miscellaneous things the group may need, one student may be responsible for getting the photos for the photo requirement, one person may be responsible for making a cover for the finished booklet, etc. You may decide within your own groups what each person's additional assignment will be.

TIMETABLE

You will have the rest of this class period to begin working. In the next class period, we will go to the library so you have access to those resources if you need them, and you may continue your project work there. After that, you will have about a week to get your information together, to get your research done. At that time, you will have one class period to pool your information, decide what will go in your section and decide how you will arrange your information in your section. Also at that time, you will submit your entry for the cover of the booklet. The class will look at all the entries and vote on which one will be used as the actual cover of the booklet. A couple of days after that, you will have to bring your completed sections to class so we can combine all of the sections into a booklet.

REMINDER   You do have to do a nonfiction reading assignment with this *Our Town* unit. You may use the reading you do for this project to fulfill that requirement if you wish. Remember to fill out your Nonfiction Reading Assignment sheet.

PROJECT WORKSHEET - *Our Town*

Section of the booklet this group is doing: _____

Names of the group members:

_____   _____

_____   _____

_____   _____

Things That Have To Be Done	Who Is Responsible?	Completion Date

WRITING ASSIGNMENT #1 - *Our Town*

PROMPT

You have to do a certain amount of research about your topic for the Project Assignment. Also, your group has to create a section of the booklet the class is making. One way for you to create your section of the booklet is to have each person in your group summarize his/her research. Then, when you go to put your section of the booklet together, you can just use this series of summaries.

For example, in the History Group Student 1 writes about the founding date to FD+25. She/he can use the dates for the heading of her/his summary, and write a summary of what happened in those years. That would be followed by the summary from Student 2 who has the years following Student 1, and so on. This same principle will work for all of the groups. Important People group members should write a summary for each of the important people they research, and simply put the person's name as the heading for each composition. In the Things To Do group, students should head their compositions with the category (museums, special events, amusement parks, etc.). In the Landmarks group, students should head their compositions with the name of the landmark about which they are reporting. Get the idea? That way, each group member contributes to the writing of the section being contributed by the group.

Your assignment, then, is to write a summary (or a series of summaries) about the topic(s) you are researching for your group.

PREWRITING

The Project Assignment pages give you a lot of good information about how to get started and do the research needed before you can actually begin writing your composition. Review the information there.

DRAFTING

Put a heading (title) at the top of (each of) your composition(s). Write approximately one to three paragraphs telling what you found in your research about that topic. If you were assigned three topics to research, you will have three compositions that are each one to three paragraphs long. If you were assigned Mexican food restaurants, for example, you should write one to three paragraphs about each of the Mexican food restaurants in your area. Each restaurant will have it's own heading.

PROMPT

When you finish the rough draft of your paper, ask a student who sits near you to read it. After reading your rough draft, he/she should tell you what he/she liked best about your work, which parts were difficult to understand, and ways in which your work could be improved. Reread your paper considering your critic's comments, and make the corrections you think are necessary. Do a final proofreading of your paper double-checking your grammar, spelling, organization, and the clarity of your ideas.

LESSONS FOUR AND FIVE

Objectives
1. To read Act One
2. To give students practice reading orally
3. To evaluate students' oral reading

Activity
Have students read their assigned parts for Act One of *Our Town* out loud in class. If you have not yet completed an oral reading evaluation for your students this marking period, this would be a good opportunity to do so. A form is included with this unit for your convenience.

LESSON SIX

Objectives
1. To review the main ideas and events from Act One
2. To preview the study questions and vocabulary for Act Two
3. To give students practice writing to express their own opinions
4. To give the teacher the opportunity to evaluate students' writing skills
5. To introduce one main theme from the play

Activity #1
Give students a few minutes to formulate answers for the study guide questions for Act One, and then discuss the answers to the questions in detail. Write the answers on the board or overhead transparency so students can have the correct answers for study purposes. Note: It is a good practice in public speaking and leadership skills for individual students to take charge of leading the discussions of the study questions. Perhaps a different student could go to the front of the class and lead the discussion each day that the study questions are discussed during this unit. Of course, the teacher should guide the discussion when appropriate and be sure to fill in any gaps the students leave.

Activity #2
Give students about fifteen minutes to preview the study questions for Act Two of *Our Town* and to do the related vocabulary work.

Activity #3
Distribute Writing Assignment #2. Discuss the directions in detail and give students ample time to complete the assignment.

ORAL READING EVALUATION - *Our Town*

Name _____ Class____ Date _____

SKILL	EXCELLENT	GOOD	AVERAGE	FAIR	POOR
Fluency	5	4	3	2	1
Clarity	5	4	3	2	1
Audibility	5	4	3	2	1
Pronunciation	5	4	3	2	1
_____	5	4	3	2	1
_____	5	4	3	2	1

Total _____   Grade _____

Comments:

WRITING ASSIGNMENT #2 - *Our Town*

PROMPT

The life cycle is a major theme in *Our Town*. People are born, they grow up, usually fall in love, get married, have children of their own, later become grandparents, and eventually die. We all know what life is like; we live our lives every day. The unknown factor is death. All of us know someone who had died, and we know that eventually we will die, too.

Most people don't like to talk about or even think about the fact that they won't live forever, much less consider the prospects of what it might be like after death. Some people believe in Heaven and Hell; others believe that there is nothing after life; still others believe in reincarnation (that we come back as someone or something else). In Act Three, Thornton Wilder gives us a glimpse of what he thinks it might be like to be dead. This may seem like a morbid assignment, but your assignment is to tell what you think happens to people after they die.

You may write a composition, a poem, or song lyrics--or if you know of a written poem, song, or passage that expresses your views, you may quote that poem, song or passage and then explain how or why it matches your own opinions. This is a very loosely structured assignment. There is no "right" or "wrong" answer to be graded. You will simply be graded on how clearly your opinions are expressed; how effectively your point is communicated.

PREWRITING

You have already given this matter some thought at some time in the past. Stop and think for a minute to recall or sort out the ideas you have. Jot them down on a piece of paper. Decide on a form in which to express your ideas (composition, poem, lyrics, etc.). Organize your ideas into a logical sequence.

DRAFTING

Whatever form you choose to use, you should have an introduction in which you introduce the idea, a body of information in which you express your ideas, and a conclusion in which you draw your thoughts to a close. If you are doing poetry or lyrics, you should title your work.

PROOFREADING

Because of the nature of this assignment, you may not want other students to read your work to help you proofread. That's okay. Just give your work a good look and carefully check it yourself.

LESSON SEVEN

<u>Objective</u>
   To read Act Two

<u>Activity</u>
   Have students read their assigned speaking parts orally.

LESSON EIGHT

<u>Objectives</u>
   1. To review the main ideas and events from Act Two
   2. To preview the study questions and vocabulary work for Act Three
   3. To practice the speaking parts for Act Three

<u>Activity #1</u>
   Give students a few minutes to formulate answers for the study guide questions for Act Two, and then discuss the answers to the questions in detail. Write the answers on the board or overhead transparency so students can have the correct answers for study purposes.

<u>Activity #2</u>
   Give students about twenty minutes to preview the study questions and do the vocabulary for Act Three.

<u>Activity #3</u>
   Let students use the remaining time in class to practice their speaking parts for Act Three.

LESSON NINE

<u>Objective</u>
   To read Act Three

<u>Activity</u>
   Have students read their assigned speaking parts orally.

LESSON TEN

Objectives
1. To review the main ideas and events from Act Three
2. To discuss *Our Town* on interpretive and critical levels

Activity #1
Take a few minutes at the beginning of the period to review the study questions for Act Three.

Activity #2
Choose the questions from the Extra Discussion Questions/Writing Assignments which seem most appropriate for your students. A class discussion of these questions is most effective if students have been given the opportunity to formulate answers to the questions prior to the discussion. To this end, you may either have all the students formulate answers to all the questions, divide your class into groups and assign one or more questions to each group, or you could assign one question to each student in your class. The option you choose will make a difference in the amount of class time needed for this activity.

Activity #3
After students have had ample time to formulate answers to the questions, begin your class discussion of the questions and the ideas presented by the questions. Be sure students take notes during the discussion so they have information to study for the unit test.

EXTRA WRITING ASSIGNMENTS/DISCUSSION QUESTIONS - *Our Town*

Interpretation

1. Describe Grover's Corners.

2. Where is the climax of the play? Explain why.

3. What is the setting of *Our Town*? Why did Thornton Wilder choose to use this setting? What does it add to the play?

4. What are the main conflicts in the play? Are they resolved? If so, how? If not, why not?

Critical

5. Does this play have a central character, a main character? If so, who is it? If not, why not?

6. Are the characters' actions believably motivated? Explain why or why not.

7. What function does the character of Howie Newsome serve in the play?

8. Characterize Thornton Wilder's style of writing. How does it contribute to the value of the play?

9. Compare the Gibbs family and the Webb family.

10. Are the characters in *Our Town* stereotypes? If so, explain why Thornton Wilder used stereotypes. If not, explain how the characters merit individuality.

11. What is the function of the Stage Manager? Is the Stage Manager necessary? Why or why not?

12. Compare and contrast George and Emily.

13. Mrs. Soames said, "Wasn't life awful --- and wonderful." Why is this a statement instead of a question? What did she mean?

14. Why was Professor Willard included in the play?

15. Life and death are major themes throughout the play. Find subtle (or not so subtle) examples of these themes in Act One and Act Two.

Our Town Extra Discussion Questions Page 2

Personal Response

16. *Our Town* won the Pulitzer Prize in 1938. Why? What's so special about this play?

17. Emily's wedding was a typical, small town wedding. If you hope to get married one day, describe what you hope your wedding will be like. If you do not want to get married, describe what you think the perfect wedding would be (for someone else!).

18. Define "success." What makes a successful life?

19. Describe the pros and cons of living where you do, whether in a small town, a city or a rural area.

20. Does *Our Town* give an accurate picture of life in the early 1900's in America? How or why not?

21. Does *Our Town* reflect an accurate picture of life in the late 1900's in America (America today)? If not, what would you change to make the play accurately reflect the present time?

LESSON ELEVEN

Objective
    To review all of the vocabulary work done in this unit

Activity
    Choose one (or more) of the vocabulary review activities listed below and spend your class period as directed in the activity. Some of the materials for these review activities are located in the Extra Activities Packet in this unit.

VOCABULARY REVIEW ACTIVITIES

1. Divide your class into two teams and have an old-fashioned spelling or definition bee.

2. Give each of your students (or students in groups of two, three or four) an *Our Town* Vocabulary Word Search Puzzle. The person (group) to find all of the vocabulary words in the puzzle first wins.

3. Give students an *Our Town* Vocabulary Word Search Puzzle without the word list. The person or group to find the most vocabulary words in the puzzle wins.

4. Use an *Our Town* Vocabulary Crossword Puzzle. Put the puzzle onto a transparency on the overhead projector (so everyone can see it), and do the puzzle together as a class.

5. Give students an *Our Town* Vocabulary Matching Worksheet to do.

6. Divide your class into two teams. Use the *Our Town* vocabulary words with their letters jumbled as a word list. Student 1 from Team A faces off against Student 1 from Team B. You write the first jumbled word on the board. The first student (1A or 1B) to unscramble the word wins the chance for his/her team to score points. If 1A wins the jumble, go to student 2A and give him/her a definition. He/she must give you the correct spelling of the vocabulary word which fits that definition. If he/she does, Team A scores a point, and you give student 3A a definition for which you expect a correctly spelled matching vocabulary word. Continue giving Team A definitions until some team member makes an incorrect response. An incorrect response sends the game back to the jumbled-word face off, this time with students 2A and 2B. Instead of repeating giving definitions to the first few students of each team, continue with the student after the one who gave the last incorrect response on the team. For example, if Team B wins the jumbled-word face-off, and student 5B gave the last incorrect answer for Team B, you would start this round of definition questions with student 6B, and so on. The team with the most points wins!

7. Have students write a story in which they correctly use as many vocabulary words as possible. Have students read their compositions orally! Post the most original compositions on your bulletin board!

LESSON TWELVE

Objectives
1. To give students time to work on their project assignments
2. To give students individual attention regarding their writing
3. To choose a cover for the finished booklet.

Activities

Collect the entries for the cover of the booklet. Show all of the entries to the class and let the class choose which one they think is best. Be sure to have copies of the chosen cover made for each student by Lesson Fifteen.

Give students this class period to work on their project assignments. Students should have their research and writing assignments done. Today the group members should be reading each others' work and figuring out how to organize the information into their sections for the *Our Town* booklet.

While students are working on these projects, call individual students to your desk or some other private area to discuss their Writing Assignment #2 compositions. A writing evaluation form is included in this unit to help you structure these writing conferences if you would like to use it.

LESSON THIRTEEN

Objectives
1. To widen the breadth of students' knowledge about the topics discussed or touched upon in *Our Town*
2. To check students' nonfiction reading assignments

Activity

Ask each student to give a brief oral report about the nonfiction work he/she read for the nonfiction reading assignment. Your criteria for evaluating this report will vary depending on the level of your students. You may wish for students to give a complete report without using notes of any kind, or you may want students to read directly from a written report, or you may want to do something in between these two extremes. Just make students aware of your criteria in ample time for them to prepare their reports.

Start with one student's report. After that, ask if anyone else in the class has read about a topic related to the first student's report. If no one has, choose another student at random. After each report, be sure to ask if anyone has a report related to the one just completed. That will help keep a continuity during the discussion of the reports.

LESSON FOURTEEN

Objectives
1. To give students the opportunity to practice writing to persuade
2. To give the teacher the opportunity to evaluate students' writing skills

Activity

Distribute Writing Assignment #3. Discuss the directions in detail and give students ample time to complete the assignment.

WRITING EVALUATION FORM - *Our Town*

Name _____ Date _____

      Grade _____

Circle One For Each Item:

Character Analysis:	excellent	good fair poor
Grammar:	correct	errors noted on paper
Spelling:	correct	errors noted on paper
Punctuation:	correct	errors noted on paper
Legibility:	excellent	good fair poor

Strengths:

Weaknesses:

Comments/Suggestions:

WRITING ASSIGNMENT #3 - *Our Town*

PROMPT

You have some understanding of what life was like in the early 1900's in America through reading *Our Town*, and you know how things are today. Your assignment is to persuade me that life is better today than it was about 100 years ago, that life is NOT better today than it was 100 years ago, OR that it is neither better nor worse--just different than it was 100 years ago. Choose ONE viewpoint and write a composition convincing me of your point.

PREWRITING

Get out two pieces of scratch paper. Divide each paper into two columns. On each paper, label the left column "Good" and the right column "Bad." One paper is for 100 years ago and one paper is for today. Start with your 100 years ago paper. In the "Good" column write down everything that was good about people's way of life then. In the "Bad" column write down everything that was bad about people's lives then. Do the same with the paper for today.

After you have finished, look at each of your papers. Decide whether life was better 100 years ago or is better today--or whether neither is better.

DRAFTING

Start with a paragraph in which you introduce the idea that 100 years ago was better, today is better or neither is better.

In the body of your paper, write at least three paragraphs, one paragraph for each of three reasons why you chose the opinion stated in your introduction. Each paragraph should have a topic sentence stating your reason, followed by specific examples supporting your statement.

End your composition with a concluding paragraph.

PROOFREADING

When you finish the rough draft of your paper, ask a student who sits near you to read it. After reading your rough draft, he/she should tell you what he/she liked best about your work, which parts were difficult to understand, and ways in which your work could be improved. Reread your paper considering your critic's comments, and make the corrections you think are necessary.

PROOFREADING

Do a final proofreading of your paper double-checking your grammar, spelling, organization, and the clarity of your ideas.

LESSON FIFTEEN

Objectives
1. To complete the project assignment
2. To expose all students to all the information collected about their town
3. To put the booklet sections together

Activity #1
Write up on the board a list of all the sections that will be in the booklet. Have students decide which would be the best order for the sections to be presented in the booklet.

Have one member from each group distribute one copy of the section his/her group made to each of the students in the class. Also distribute one copy of the cover to each student in the class.

Have students organize and put together their booklets.

Activity #2
Look through the booklet with your students. You may wish to have students read their own sections orally, or you may give students time to read silently--however you think your students will most benefit from the exercise. The point is to make all students familiar with all of the information in the booklet.

Activity #3
Ask each student to make a list of ten questions for which answers can be found in the booklet. Tell them to make an answer key on a separate sheet of paper. Have students exchange their lists of ten questions and look up the answers in the booklet. They should exchange papers back with the student they originally made the exchange. Since the student who wrote the questions has the answer key, he/she should grade the exercise. Answer keys and exercises should be handed in together to the teacher.

LESSON SIXTEEN

Objective
    To review the main ideas presented in *Our Town*

Activity #1
    Choose one of the review games/activities included in the packet and spend your class period as outlined there. Some materials for these activities are located in the Unit Resources section of this unit.

Activity #2
    Remind students that the Unit Test will be in the next class meeting. Stress the review of the Study Guides and their class notes as a last minute, brush-up review for homework.

REVIEW GAMES/ACTIVITIES - *Our Town*

1. Ask the class to make up a unit test for *Our Town*. The test should have 4 sections: matching, true/false, short answer, and essay. Students may use 1/2 period to make the test and then swap papers and use the other 1/2 class period to take a test a classmate has devised. (open book) You may want to use the unit test included in this packet or take questions from the students' unit tests to formulate your own test.

2. Take 1/2 period for students to make up true and false questions (including the answers). Collect the papers and divide the class into two teams. Draw a big tic-tac-toe board on the chalk board. Make one team X and one team O. Ask questions to each side, giving each student one turn. If the question is answered correctly, that students' team's letter (X or O) is placed in the box. If the answer is incorrect, no mark is placed in the box. The object is to get three marks in a row like tic-tac-toe. You may want to keep track of the number of games won for each team.

3. Take 1/2 period for students to make up questions (true/false and short answer). Collect the questions. Divide the class into two teams. You'll alternate asking questions to individual members of teams A & B (like in a spelling bee). The question keeps going from A to B until it is correctly answered, then a new question is asked. A correct answer does not allow the team to get another question. Correct answers are +2 points; incorrect answers are -1 point.

4. Have students pair up and quiz each other from their study guides and class notes.

5. Give students a *Our Town* crossword puzzle to complete.

6. Divide your class into two teams. Use the *Our Town* crossword words with their letters jumbled as a word list. Student 1 from Team A faces off against Student 1 from Team B. You write the first jumbled word on the board. The first student (1A or 1B) to unscramble the word wins the chance for his/her team to score points. If 1A wins the jumble, go to student 2A and give him/her a clue. He/she must give you the correct word which matches that clue. If he/she does, Team A scores a point, and you give student 3A a clue for which you expect another correct response. Continue giving Team A clues until some team member makes an incorrect response. An incorrect response sends the game back to the jumbled-word face off, this time with students 2A and 2B. Instead of repeating giving clues to the first few students of each team, continue with the student after the one who gave the last incorrect response on the team. For example, if Team B wins the jumbled-word face-off, and student 5B gave the last incorrect answer for Team B, you would start this round of clue questions with student 6B, and so on. The team with the most points wins!

UNIT TESTS

SHORT ANSWER UNIT TEST 1 - *Our Town*

I. Matching/Identify

____ 1. Crowell   A. Rebecca's mother

____ 2. George   B. Doctor

____ 3. Mrs. Gibbs   C. His appendix burst

____ 4. Mrs. Webb   D. Gossipy choir member

____ 5. Rebecca   E. Had a drinking problem

____ 6. Mr. Webb   F. Delivered newspapers

____ 7. Mr. Gibbs   G. Emily's cousin

____ 8. Wally   H. Emily's mother

____ 9. Newsome   I. Married Emily

____ 10. Soames   J. George's sister

____ 11. Stimson   K. Editor

____ 12. Sam Craig   L. Milkman

II. Short Answer

1. What functions does the stage manager serve?

2. What does Mr. Webb say about drinking, culture and social injustice in Grover's Corners?

Our Town Short Answer Unit Test 1 Page 2

3. "You've got to love life to have life, and you've got to have life to love life." What does that mean?

4. How did George and Emily decide they were "meant for each other"?

5. Which of the characters we met in Acts I and II end up in the cemetery, and how did each die?

6. How does the stage manager describe death?

7. How does Emily describe the living?

8. Mrs. Gibbs says, "Choose the least important day of your life. It will be important enough." What does she mean?

Our Town Short Answer Unit Test 1 Page 3

9. How did the day of Emily's twelfth birthday begin as compared to the days in Act I and Act II?

10. Emily says, "They don't understand, do they?" Who are "they," and what don't they understand?

III. Composition

What is the point of *Our Town*? When we read books, we usually come away from our reading experience a little richer, having given more thought to a particular aspect of life. What do you think Thornton Wilder intended us to gain from reading his play?

Our Town Short Answer Unit Test 1 Page 4

IV. Vocabulary
    Listen to the vocabulary words and write them down.
    Go back later and fill in the correct definition for each word.

1.

2.

3.

4.

5.

6.

7.

8.

9.

10.

SHORT ANSWER UNIT TEST 2 - *Our Town*

I. Matching

____ 1. Crowell   A. Delivered newspapers

____ 2. George   B. Emily's cousin

____ 3. Mrs. Gibbs   C. Emily's mother

____ 4. Mrs. Webb   D. Married Emily

____ 5. Rebecca   E. George's sister

____ 6. Mr. Webb   F. Editor

____ 7. Mr. Gibbs   G. Doctor

____ 8. Wally   H. His appendix burst

____ 9. Newsome   I. Milkman

____ 10. Soames   J. Had a drinking problem

____ 11. Stimson   K. Rebecca's mother

____ 12. Sam Craig   L. Gossipy choir member

II. Short Answer

1. What do you notice is different about this play as opposed to others you may be familiar with? Why do you think the author made these changes?

2. Why does Mrs. Soames talk about Simon Stimson?

Our Town Short Answer Unit Test 2 Page 2

3. "Everybody has a right to their own troubles." Explain.

4. What was the "topic" of Act II? What characters were the center of attention? Why?

5. The stage manager says that dead people get "weaned away from earth." They gradually lose interest in the things they had and people they loved. What things in Act Three support this idea?

6. Emily describes the living by saying, "They're sort-of shut-up in little boxes." What does she mean?

7. Mrs. Gibbs comments to Emily meaning that even the least important days of our lives are full of things we should appreciate and would miss if they were gone. Every day is special because we are alive to enjoy it. Emily chose to see her 12th birthday. How did her birthday prove Mrs. Gibbs's comment?

8. "Oh, earth, you're too wonderful for anybody to realize you!" Explain what Emily is expressing here.

Our Town Short Answer Unit Test 2 Page 3

III. Composition

It has been said that the appeal of *Our Town* is based upon the basic human values found in it. What basic human values are found in this play? Be specific.

IV. Vocabulary

Listen to the vocabulary words and write them down. Go back later and fill in the correct definition for each word.

1.

2.

3.

4.

5.

6.

7.

8.

9.

10.

KEY: SHORT ANSWER UNIT TESTS - *Our Town*

The short answer questions are taken directly from the study guides.
If you need to look up the answers, you will find them in the study guide section.

Answers to the composition questions will vary depending on your
class discussions and the level of your students.

For the vocabulary section of the test, choose ten of the
words from the vocabulary lists to read orally for your students.

The answers to the matching section of the test are below.

Answers to the matching section of the Advanced Short Answer Unit Test
are the same as for Short Answer Unit Test #2.

<u>Test #1</u>
1. F
2. I
3. A
4. H
5. J
6. K
7. B
8. C
9. L
10. D
11. E
12. G

<u>Test #2</u>
1. A
2. D
3. K
4. C
5. E
6. F
7. G
8. H
9. I
10. L
11. J
12. B

ADVANCED SHORT ANSWER UNIT TEST - *Our Town*

I. Matching

____ 1. Crowell   A. Delivered newspapers

____ 2. George   B. Emily's cousin

____ 3. Mrs. Gibbs   C. Emily's mother

____ 4. Mrs. Webb   D. Married Emily

____ 5. Rebecca   E. George's sister

____ 6. Mr. Webb   F. Editor

____ 7. Mr. Gibbs   G. Doctor

____ 8. Wally   H. His appendix burst

____ 9. Newsome   I. Milkman

____ 10. Soames   J. Had a drinking problem

____ 11. Stimson   K. Rebecca's mother

____ 12. Sam Craig   L. Gossipy choir member

II. Short Answer

1. "Normal" plays have intricate sets and props, but *Our Town* does not. Why not?

2. Choose four characters Mr. Wilder uses as stereotypes. Explain who they are and why Mr. Wilder chose to use stereotypes for these characters.

Our Town Advanced Short Answer Unit Test Page 2

3. Emily is allowed to go back and relive/look at one day from her life. What does Mr. Wilder achieve by using this technique?

4. There are at least three views of life presented in *Our Town*: a view from the living, a view from the recently deceased, and a view from the long dead. Explain how the living see life, how the recently deceased see life, and how the long dead see life.

5. Is *Our Town* considered a tragedy in the literary sense of the word? Why or why not?

Our Town Advanced Short Answer Unit Test Page 3

6. What makes this play about ordinary things extraordinary?

7. Thornton Wilder divided his play into three acts. What was the topic and main point of each act?

8. Was the stage manager necessary? What were his duties?

9. Emily says, "They don't understand, do they?" Who are "they" and what don't they understand?

Our Town Advanced Short Answer Unit Test Page 4

III. Composition

This play was first produced in 1938 and was written about life in the early 1900's in America. Even if you did not know these facts, you would be able to estimate both facts from reading the text. Using your knowledge of the text and your knowledge of world events, explain what things in the text tell us or give us clues that the play was written about the early 1900's and that the play was written prior to the 1960's.

Our Town Advanced Short Answer Unit Test Page 5

IV. Vocabulary
    Write down the vocabulary words you are given.
    Go back later and use all of those vocabulary words in a composition relating to *Our Town*.

MULTIPLE CHOICE UNIT TEST 1 - *Our Town*

I. Matching

____ 1. Crowell   A. Rebecca's mother

____ 2. George   B. Doctor

____ 3. Mrs. Gibbs   C. His appendix burst

____ 4. Mrs. Webb   D. Gossipy choir member

____ 5. Rebecca   E. Had a drinking problem

____ 6. Mr. Webb   F. Delivered newspapers

____ 7. Mr. Gibbs   G. Emily's cousin

____ 8. Wally   H. Emily's mother

____ 9. Newsome   I. Married Emily

____ 10. Soames   J. George's sister

____ 11. Stimson   K. Editor

____ 12. Sam Craig   L. Milkman

II. Multiple Choice

1. The stage manager serves many functions. Which of these is not one of them?
    a. Giving the audience background information.
    b. Presenting the author's view on many issues.
    c. Making sure the audience can see and hear the actors.
    d. Bringing the audience into the play, making it easier for them to identify the setting with their own town.

2. What seems to be the point of the first act?
    a. The point is to foreshadow the action of the later acts.
    b. The point is to show the contrast between appearance and reality in their lives.
    c. The point is to introduce the characters and show them in their ordinary daily lives.
    d. The point is to build suspense for the dramatic conclusion to come.

Our Town Multiple Choice Unit Test 1 Page 2

3. Which of these lines from the play can be interpreted to mean that one has to appreciate life to make life fuller; when one doesn't have life anymore, one can't appreciate life as one could have when alive?
    a. "There isn't much culture, but maybe this is the place to tell you that we've got a lot of pleasures of a kind here; we like the sun comin' up over the mountain in the morning, and we notice a good deal about the birds."
    b. "You've got to love life to have life, and you've got to have life to love life.
    c. We're all hunting like everybody else for a way the diligent and sensible can rise to the top and the lazy and quarrelsome can sink to the bottom.
    d. Now there are some things we all know, but we don't take'm out and look at'm very often. We all know that something is eternal...and that something has to do with human beings.

4. "Everybody has a right to their own troubles." How are troubles seen in the context of the play.
    a. They are seen as a great burden.
    b. They are seen as some of those little things people don't appreciate; as a contrast to the good times.
    c. They are seen as the backbone of character building.
    d. They are seen as folly caused by people's own humanity.

5. George and Emily decided that they were "meant for each other" for several reasons. Which of the following is not one of the reasons?
    a. They had been admiring each other from afar for some time.
    b. They were born on the same day in the same year, were the same height, and had the same general average in high school.
    c. Emily had been helping George with his schoolwork earlier.
    d. George realized that if Emily thought enough of him to bring a flaw in his character to his attention, that she must really care for him.

6. What was the "topic" of Act II?
    a. It was birth and death.
    b. It was the sameness of life.
    c. It was love and marriage.
    d. It was the importance of children.

Our Town Multiple Choice Unit Test 1 Page 3

7. How does the stage manager describe death?
    a. He says that dead people get "weaned away from earth." They gradually lose interest in the things they had and the people they loved.
    b. He says that most people leave the world kicking and screaming, just the way they come into it.
    c. He says that death is a highly personal experience, and can't really be accurately described except by the person who is dying, so we will never really know what it is like.
    d. He is very matter-of-fact, and says it is just a part of life.

8. A new character, Sam Craig, was introduced in Act Three. What was his function?
    a. The author is setting the play up so that we can write a sequel if this first one is well-received by the audience.
    b. It is a symbolism that things change.
    c. While the character is being filled in on background information, so is the audience.
    d. His function is to bring Grover's Corners into the modern world.

9. Emily says, "they're sort of shut up in little boxes." Whom is she describing?
    a. She is describing the living.
    b. She is describing the dead.
    c. She is describing her brother's pet bugs.
    d. She is joking about how birthday and wedding presents must feel inside their boxes. In the play, the little boxes are symbols of people's small minds and petty problems.

10. Emily says, "I never realized before how troubled and how . . . how in the dark live persons are." What does she mean?
    a. Now that she is in heaven, she is happy and her troubles are over.
    b. She was in a state of denial when she was alive, and thought everyone else was perfect.
    c. People get so busy with their own thoughts, ambitions and problems that they don't take time to open themselves up to try and see, understand, and appreciate everything in the world.
    d. Death brings insight that life couldn't possibly give.

11. What did Emily say about life?
    a. "Ignorance and blindness are all there really is."
    b. "The strain's so bad that every sixteen hours everybody lies down and gets a rest."
    c. "Oh, earth, you're too wonderful for anybody to realize you!"
    d. "There are some surprises waiting for you on the table.

Our Town Multiple Choice Unit Test 1 Page 4

12. "Mother Gibbs," said Emily, ". . . They don't understand, do they?" What don't they understand, and who are "they"?
    a. They are the audience, and they don't understand the true meaning of the play.
    b. They are the poor souls who died without the salvation of religion.
    c. They are the living who don't understand the importance of enjoying every moment of life.
    d. They are the relatives of the deceased. They don't understand how happy the dead are to be free of the burden of life.

III. Composition

Create five more multiple choice questions (complete with correct answers and distractors) which show your knowledge of the play *Our Town*. The questions cannot be character identification related (for example, "Howie Newsome was a. the paperboy b. the milkman c. a friend of Emily d. a member of the baseball team"). The questions must be related to the <u>ideas</u> presented in the play. Circle the correct answers.

Our Town Multiple Choice Unit Test 1 Page 5

IV. Vocabulary

___ 1. Eternal	a. Vain; holding an unusually high opinion of oneself

___ 2. Anguished	b. Prickly, weed-like plant with purple flower

___ 3. Affronted	c. Gloominess; ridiculously dismal

___ 4. Legacy	d. Agonized; tormented

___ 5. Bereaved	e. Spreading rumors or talk of a personal or sensational nature

___ 6. Exasperation	f. An interlude during a scene when all performers freeze momentarily

___ 7. Scandal	g. Structures used for supporting vines & creeping plants

___ 8. Burgle	h. Flowers native to Peru, having fragrant, purple flowers

___ 9. Burdock	i. In a short or brusque manner

___ 10. Conceited	j. Lasting forever

___ 11. Lugubriousness	k. Intentionally insulted

___ 12. Diligent	l. Marked by persevering, painstaking effort

___ 13. Silicate	m. Violation of another's rights or of what is right

___ 14. Heliotrope	n. Suffering the loss of a loved one

___ 15. Contriving	o. Compound containing silicon, oxygen and one or more metals

___ 16. Injustice	p. An incident that brings about disgrace or offends society

___ 17. Trellises	q. Steal

___ 18. Abruptly	r. Something handed down from an ancestor

___ 19. Tableau	s. Feeling of impatient anger or annoyance

___ 20. Gossiping	t. Planning with cleverness or ingenuity

MULTIPLE CHOICE UNIT TEST 2 - *Our Town*

I. Matching

____ 1. Crowell   A. Delivered newspapers

____ 2. George   B. Emily's cousin

____ 3. Mrs. Gibbs   C. Emily's mother

____ 4. Mrs. Webb   D. Married Emily

____ 5. Rebecca   E. George's sister

____ 6. Mr. Webb   F. Editor

____ 7. Mr. Gibbs   G. Doctor

____ 8. Wally   H. His appendix burst

____ 9. Newsome   I. Milkman

____ 10. Soames   J. Had a drinking problem

____ 11. Stimson   K. Rebecca's mother

____ 12. Sam Craig   L. Gossipy choir member

II. Multiple Choice

1. The stage manager serves many functions. Which of these is not one of them?
    a. Giving the audience background information.
    b. Presenting the author's view on many issues.
    c. Bringing the audience into the play, making it easier for them to identify the setting with their own town.
    d. Making sure the audience can see and hear the actors.

2. What seems to be the point of the first act?
    a. The point is to introduce the characters and show them in their ordinary daily lives.
    b. The point is to show the contrast between appearance and reality in their lives.
    c. The point is to foreshadow the action of the later acts.
    d. The point is to build suspense for the dramatic conclusion to come.

Our Town Multiple Choice Unit Test 2 Page 2

3. Which of these lines from the play can be interpreted to mean that one has to appreciate life to make life fuller; when one doesn't have life anymore, one can't appreciate life as one could have when alive?
    a. "There isn't much culture, but maybe this is the place to tell you that we've got a lot of pleasures of a kind here; we like the sun comin' up over the mountain in the morning, and we notice a good deal about the birds."
    b. Now there are some things we all know, but we don't take'm out and look at'm very often. We all know that something is eternal...and that something has to do with human beings.
    c. We're all hunting like everybody else for a way the diligent and sensible can rise to the top and the lazy and quarrelsome can sink to the bottom.
    d. "You've got to love life to have life, and you've got to have life to love life.

4. "Everybody has a right to their own troubles." How are troubles seen in the context of the play.
    a. They are seen as a great burden.
    b. They are seen as the backbone of character building.
    c. They are seen as some of those little things people don't appreciate; as a contrast to the good times.
    d. They are seen as folly caused by people's own humanity.

5. George and Emily decided that they were "meant for each other" for several reasons. Which of the following is not one of the reasons?
    a. They had been admiring each other from afar for some time.
    b. Emily had been helping George with his schoolwork earlier.
    c. They were born on the same day in the same year, were the same height, and had the same general average in high school.
    d. George realized that if Emily thought enough of him to bring a flaw in his character to his attention, that she must really care for him.

6. What was the "topic" of Act II?
    a. It was birth and death.
    b. It was love and marriage.
    c. It was the sameness of life.
    d. It was the importance of children.

Our Town Multiple Choice Unit Test 2 Page 3

7. How does the stage manager describe death?
    a. He says that most people leave the world kicking and screaming, just the way they come into it.
    b. He says that dead people get "weaned away from earth." They gradually lose interest in the things they had and the people they loved.
    c. He says that death is a highly personal experience, and can't really be accurately described except by the person who is dying, so we will never really know what it is like.
    d. He is very matter-of-fact, and says it is just a part of life.

8. A new character, Sam Craig, was introduced in Act Three. What was his function?
    a. The author is setting the play up so that we can write a sequel if this first one is well-received by the audience.
    b. It is a symbolism that things change.
    c. His function is to bring Grover's Corners into the modern world.
    d. While the character is being filled in on background information, so is the audience.

9. Emily says, "they're sort of shut up in little boxes." Whom is she describing?
    a. She is describing her brother's pet bugs.
    b. She is describing the dead.
    c. She is describing the living.
    d. She is joking about how birthday and wedding presents must feel inside their boxes. In the play, the little boxes are symbols of people's small minds and petty problems.

10. Emily says, "I never realized before how troubled and how . . . how in the dark live persons are." What does she mean?
    a. Now that she is in heaven, she is happy and her troubles are over.
    b. She was in a state of denial when she was alive, and thought everyone else was perfect.
    c. Death brings insight that life couldn't possibly give.
    d. People get so busy with their own thoughts, ambitions and problems that they don't take time to open themselves up to try and see, understand, and appreciate everything in the world.

11. What did Emily say about life?
    a. "Oh, earth, you're too wonderful for anybody to realize you!"
    b. "The strain's so bad that every sixteen hours everybody lies down and gets a rest."
    c. "Ignorance and blindness are all there really is."
    d. "There are some surprises waiting for you on the table."

Our Town Multiple Choice Unit Test 2 Page 4

12. "Mother Gibbs," said Emily, ". . . They don't understand, do they?" What don't they understand, and who are "they"?
    a. They are the audience, and they don't understand the true meaning of the play.
    b. They are the living who don't understand the importance of enjoying every moment of life.
    c. They are the poor souls who died without the salvation of religion.
    d. They are the relatives of the deceased. They don't understand how happy the dead are to be free of the burden of life.

III. Composition

You are Emily. You have died, but you have gone back to earth to leave a letter for your child. Knowing what you now know, write the letter Emily would write to her child.

Our Town Multiple Choice Unit Test 2 Page 5

IV. Vocabulary

___ 1. Contriving   a. Compound containing silicon, oxygen and one or more metals

___ 2. Diligent   b. In a nasty way intending to hurt someone

___ 3. Heliotrope   c. Feeling of impatient anger or annoyance

___ 4. Silicate   d. Planning with cleverness or ingenuity

___ 5. Injustice   e. Violation of another's rights or of what is right

___ 6. Abruptly   f. Slowly detached from something one is used to having

___ 7. Phosphate   g. Intentionally insulted

___ 8. Affronted   h. Frowning in anger or disapproval

___ 9. Weaned   i. Dejected; dispirited or depressed

___ 10. Legacy   j. Something handed down from an ancestor

___ 11. Anguished   k. Suffering the loss of a loved one

___ 12. Proscenium   l. Flowers native to Peru, having fragrant, purple flowers

___ 13. Conceited   m. Vain; holding an usually high opinion of oneself

___ 14. Bereaved   n. In a short or brusque manner

___ 15. Exasperation   o. Having no particular interest or concern for

___ 16. Scowling   p. Marked by persevering, painstaking effort

___ 17. Scandal   q. Stage area between curtain and orchestra

___ 18. Crestfallen   r. An incident that brings about disgrace or offends society

___ 19. Indifferent   s. Agonized; tormented

___ 20. Bitingly   t. A soda fountain drink with carbonated water & flavored syrup

ANSWER SHEET - *Our Town*
Multiple Choice Unit Tests

I. Matching
1. ___
2. ___
3. ___
4. ___
5. ___
6. ___
7. ___
8. ___
9. ___
10. ___
11. ___
12. ___

II. Multiple Choice
1. ___
2. ___
3. ___
4. ___
5. ___
6. ___
7. ___
8. ___
9. ___
10. ___
11. ___
12. ___

IV. Vocabulary
1. ___
2. ___
3. ___
4. ___
5. ___
6. ___
7. ___
8. ___
9. ___
10. ___
11. ___
12. ___
13. ___
14. ___
15. ___
16. ___
17. ___
18. ___
19. ___
20. ___

ANSWER KEY - *Our Town*
Multiple Choice Unit Tests

Answers to Unit Test 1 are in the left column. Answers to Unit Test 2 are in the right column.

I. Matching	II. Multiple Choice	IV. Vocabulary
1. F A	1. C D	1. J D
2. I D	2. C A	2. D P
3. A K	3. B D	3. K L
4. H C	4. B C	4. R A
5. J E	5. B C	5. N E
6. K F	6. C B	6. S N
7. B G	7. A B	7. P T
8. C H	8. C D	8. Q G
9. L I	9. A C	9. B F
10. D L	10. C D	10. A J
11. E J	11. C A	11. C S
12. G B	12. C B	12. L Q
		13. O M
		14. H K
		15. T C
		16. M H
		17. G R
		18. I I
		19. F O
		20. E B

UNIT RESOURCE MATERIALS

BULLETIN BOARD IDEAS - *Our Town*

1. Save one corner of the board for the best of students' *Our Town* writing assignments.

2. Take one of the word search puzzles from the extra activities packet and with a marker copy it over in a large size on the bulletin board. Write the clue words to find to one side. Invite students prior to and after class to find the words and circle them on the bulletin board.

3. Write several of the most significant quotations from the play onto the board on brightly colored paper.

4. Make a bulletin board listing the vocabulary words for this unit. As you complete sections of the play and discuss the vocabulary for each section, write the definitions on the bulletin board. (If your board is one students face frequently, it will help them learn the words.)

5. Title the board: OUR TOWN. Find pictures--photographs--of your town, your neighborhood and place them on the board on colorful paper. Check with your newspaper or yearbook staff to see if they have any extra pictures. You might check with the library or local newspaper. Students may want to bring in pictures to contribute to the board. Otherwise, you may want to take a camera out around town and snap a few of your own pictures of people and places everyone associates with your town.

6. Snip (or have students snip) interesting articles from your local newspaper(s) telling about your town, the things going on there, and the people. Post these on the board.

7. Do a bulletin board about dealing with the death of loved ones. This could be done in conjunction with an in-class guest speaker on the topic.

8. As an introductory activity, have students create a "daily routine" for your town. Write this up on the bulletin board. Perhaps write the daily routine from Grover's Corners up on the board, too and compare and contrast it with your town's.

9. Let each student write one thing he/she most appreciates but least often recognizes in his/her own life. If you have a small class, go around the room two or three times and let students write up more.

10. Title your board OUR TOWN. Divide the board into three sections: DAILY LIFE, LOVE AND MARRIAGE, and DEATH. Post pictures that are appropriate for each phase of life.

EXTRA ACTIVITIES

One of the difficulties in teaching a play is that all students don't read at the same speed. One student who likes to read may take the play home and finish it in a day or two. Sometimes a few students finish the in-class assignments early. The problem, then, is finding suitable extra activities for students.

The best thing I've found is to keep a little library in the classroom. For this unit on *Our Town,* you might check out from the school library other related books and articles about your own town's history, current events, and important people who live and have lived in your town. Articles about different cultures' beliefs regarding death and burial rites would be interesting. Reviews of *Our Town* or biographical information about Thornton Wilder would also be appropriate. Any information you might be able to find about ways to deal with the death or other permanent loss of a loved one would be helpful.

Other things you may keep on hand are puzzles. We have made some relating directly to *Our Town* for you. Feel free to duplicate them.

Some students may like to draw. You might devise a contest or allow some extra-credit grade for students who draw characters or scenes from *Our Town.* Note, too, that if the students do not want to keep their drawings you may pick up some extra bulletin board materials this way. If you have a contest and you supply the prize (a CD or something like that perhaps), you could, possibly, make the drawing itself a non-returnable entry fee.

The pages which follow contain games, puzzles and worksheets. The keys, when appropriate, immediately follow the puzzle or worksheet. There are two main groups of activities: one group for the unit; that is, generally relating to the *Our Town* text, and another group of activities related strictly to the *Our Town* vocabulary.

Directions for these games, puzzles and worksheets are self-explanatory. The object here is to provide you with extra materials you may use in any way you choose.

MORE ACTIVITIES - *Our Town*

1. Pick a scene with a great deal of dialogue and have the students act it out on a stage. (Perhaps you could assign various scenes to different groups of students so more than one scene could be acted and more students could participate.)

2. Have students make a model of Grover's Corners or draw a map of the town as they imagine it would be. You could have them either stick only to the details given in the play -- or you could let them create the details which are not given.

3. Take your class to see a production of *Our Town*.

4. Have students design a playbill (front and back and inside) for *Our Town*.

5. Have students design a bulletin board (ready to be put up; not just sketched) for *Our Town*.

6. Have students research and report on every day life in the late 1930's, when this play was written.

7. Have students choose one act of the play (with sufficient dialogue) to rewrite as a chapter in a book. In conjunction with this assignment, have students write a composition explaining the difficulties they encountered in changing from one written form to another.

8. Divide your class into groups. Have each group plan a wedding--everything from making the invitations to deciding on a cake and reception arrangements, etc. (That's something they might need to really DO in the future!) An alternative to this would be to have two people in your class be a future bride and future groom. Divide you class into groups, one aspect of the wedding plans to be arranged by each group (one for flowers, one or dress/clothing for the event, one for reception food, one for invitations, one for reception music, one for scheduling the events of the wedding day, one for photography, etc.) Actually have a "mock wedding" and have students carry through with their plans. (They don't have to choose expensive clothes, just ordinary "dress up clothes" students might already have, for example. Food could be things that are easy to bring to class. Invitations could be hand made and xeroxed. It doesn't have to be expensive to give students the flavor of the real thing.)

9. Invite a psychologist or sociologist to come to your class to speak to students about coping with the loss of a loved one.

10. Visit a cemetery and have someone who knows a lot about it tell your class about some of the people who are buried there.

WORD SEARCH - *Our Town*

All words in this list are associated with *Our Town*. The words are placed backwards, forward, diagonally, up and down. The included words are listed below the word searches.

```
M W D B Q H S M R M T P D G Q C T E N G R X J D
J R P G Y L M Z A E O K F E K C S C A W N S Q R
W I L D E R P N E U M O N I A S R E N R O C O K
S E D I O O A C E A Y I N D W T N C L A T T C D
H R D T F G R X S W S T L S B E H D M B I H K D
F W C D E E I G N F S T F Y C X O E J D U R F X
R O L R I D W J E A M O I S R H S R E B E O L D
D M S T N N T Y E H T C M M D E I W D P S I R Y
F J R E V C G L L B G Z M E S B T L N I L K R T
Q U P V K H Y L G M G I B B S O Z E D L N L T C
S P N N G Z C K M D W Y V T R Y N D M B L A G H
A D X E N C K H C J X B T C P X M M X E I P R S
L J M W R C F G V W Q B V S M V Z T W H C R B Y
K R B V X A W M D L P T Q Q M S G O K H C P T H
L K N P X X L R Z Y B H T M B L R X S N N W W H
D M W X K T D Z C Z X Q H X G C T M L D G P X G
X D K W C C T M N S Y Z N N G K G B C M P G X R
```

ACT	DOCTOR	LIFE	SOAMES
APPENDIX	EARTH	MANAGER	STIMSON
CEMETERY	EDITOR	MOON	TOWN
CHILDBIRTH	EMILY	NEWSOME	TROUBLES
CORNERS	FUNERAL	ORDINARY	WEDDING
CRIED	GEORGE	PNEUMONIA	WILDER
CROWELL	GIBBS	SAM	DEATH
	LEAST	SCENE	

CROSSWORD - *Our Town*

CROSSWORD CLUES - *Our Town*

ACROSS
1. Our ----
3. Play division
5. Rebecca's brother
8. Craig; Mrs. Gibbs' nephew
10. Marriage vows 'I --.'
11. Mr. Gibbs is one
13. Wally Webb's burst
16. Present plural of 'to be'
17. It needs to be chopped
18. You've got to love --- to have ---
19. A bunch of baseball teams that play each other
20. George & Rebecca talk about it before going to sleep
24. His drinking problem is a scandal
26. One time
28. Belonging to him
29. Burial ceremony
31. Choose the --- important day of your life; it will be important enough.
34. Unusual
35. Author
37. What the ladies did at the wedding
38. Definite article
40. Setting for most of Act III
42. Past tense of 'to sit'
43. She married George
44. Leave something to someone via a will

DOWN
1. Everyone has a right to their own
2. Marriage ceremony
4. Delivers newspapers
6. Single
7. Mr. Webb's occupation
8. Gossipy choir member
9. Stage ---; gives audience background info
12. Grover's -----
14. Mr. Gibbs died of it
15. Milk man
21. She married George
22. Emily died during this
23. Opposite of on
25. Not unusual; routine
27. Indefinite article
30. Oh, ---, you are too wonderful for anybody to realize you!
32. Act division
33. Rebecca's last name
36. The end of one's life
37. Life ----; born, live, die
39. What the choir members did
41. 9 baseball players make up a ----
43. Final curtain falls at the ---

CROSSWORD ANSWER KEY - *Our Town*

	T	O	W	N		A	C	T				G	E	O	R	G	E	
	R		E			R		S	A	M			N			D		
D	O		D	O	C	T	O	R		O		A	P	P	E	N	D	I	X
	U		D		O		W		A		N		N			E		T
	B		I		R		E		M		A	R	E		W	O	O	D
	L		N		N		L	I	F	E		G		U		S		R
L	E	A	G	U	E		L			S		E		M	O	O	N	
	S				R				E			R		O		M		C
		O		S	T	I	M	S	O	N		O	N	C	E		H
		F		A			I		R			I			H	I	S
		F	U	N	E	R	A	L		D		L	E	A	S	T		L
	G				A		Y		I				C		O	D	D
W	I	L	D	E	R				N		C	R	I	E	D		B
	B	E		T	H	E			A		Y		N				I
	B		A		H		S		R		C	E	M	E	T	E	R	Y
	S	A	T			E	M	I	L	Y		L			E		T
			H			N		N		B	E	Q	U	E	A	T	H
						D		G						M			

MATCHING QUIZ/WORKSHEET 1 - *Our Town*

___ 1. SCENE   A. His drinking problem is a scandal

___ 2. GIBBS   B. Burial ceremony

___ 3. MOON   C. Delivers newspapers

___ 4. CEMETERY   D. Oh, ---, you are too wonderful for anybody to realize you!

___ 5. CORNERS   E. Rebecca's last name

___ 6. SAM   F. Wally Webb's burst

___ 7. STIMSON   G. The end of one's life

___ 8. LIFE   H. Emily died during this

___ 9. FUNERAL   I. Play division

___ 10. APPENDIX   J. George & Rebecca talk about it before going to sleep

___ 11. WILDER   K. Mr. Webb's occupation

___ 12. EDITOR   L. You've got to love --- to have ---

___ 13. CHILDBIRTH   M. Act Division

___ 14. DEATH   N. Grover's -----

___ 15. EARTH   O. Not unusual; routine

___ 16. ACT   P. Craig; Mrs. Gibbs' nephew

___ 17. LEAST   Q. Rebecca's brother

___ 18. GEORGE   R. Setting for most of Act III

___ 19. ORDINARY   S. Author

___ 20. CROWELL   T. Choose the --- important day of your life; it will be important enough.

MATCHING QUIZ/WORKSHEET 2 - *Our Town*

___ 1. SAM   A. Delivers newspapers

___ 2. CROWELL   B. George & Rebecca talk about it before going to sleep

___ 3. CORNERS   C. Our ----

___ 4. PNEUMONIA   D. Craig; Mrs. Gibbs' nephew

___ 5. GIBBS   E. Grover's -----

___ 6. SCENE   F. Mr. Gibbs died of it

___ 7. EMILY   G. Act division

___ 8. LIFE   H. What the ladies did at the wedding

___ 9. ORDINARY   I. She married George

___ 10. CHILDBIRTH   J. You've got to love --- to have ---

___ 11. TOWN   K. Emily died during this

___ 12. FUNERAL   L. Mr. Gibbs is one

___ 13. WEDDING   M. Rebecca's last name

___ 14. NEWSOME   N. Marriage ceremony

___ 15. WILDER   O. Not unusual; routine

___ 16. ACT   P. Setting for most of Act III

___ 17. CEMETERY   Q. Play division

___ 18. MOON   R. Author

___ 19. DOCTOR   S. Milk man

___ 20. CRIED   T. Burial ceremony

KEY: MATCHING QUIZ/WORKSHEETS - *Our Town*

Worksheet 1	Worksheet 2
1. M	1. D
2. E	2. B
3. J	3. C
4. R	4. B
5. N	5. B
6. P	6. C
7. A	7. B
8. L	8. D
9. B	9. A
10. F	10. C
11. S	11. B
12. K	12. D
13. H	13. D
14. G	14. A
15. D	15. B
16. I	16. B
17. T	17. C
18. Q	18. A
19. O	19. D
20. C	20. D

JUGGLE LETTER REVIEW GAME CLUE SHEET - *Our Town*

SCRAMBLED	WORD	CLUE
TSNOIMS	STIMSON	His drinking problem is a scandal
RROESCN	CORNERS	Grover's _____
RORADIYN	ORDINARY	Not unusual; routine
HLHRIDTCBI	CHILDBIRTH	Emily died during this
UALFERN	FUNERAL	Burial ceremony
MNSOEWE	NEWSOME	Milk man
AGRNEMA	MANAGER	Stage ____; gives audience background info
IEYML	EMILY	She married George
UEANPIMON	PNEUMONIA	Mr. Gibbs died of it
SBIBG	GIBBS	Rebecca's last name
DECRI	CRIED	What the ladies did at the wedding
IDGDNEW	WEDDING	Marriage ceremony
MSOASE	SOAMES	Gossipy choir member
OONM	MOON	George and Rebecca talk about it before going to sleep
TLEAS	LEAST	Choose the _____ important day of your life; it will be important enough
AMS	SAM	Craig; Mrs. Gibbs' nephew
RHTEA	EARTH	Oh, ____, you are too wonderful for anybody to realize you.
UOESLBTR	TROUBLES	Everyone has a right to their own
WLCOLER	CROWELL	Delivers newspapers
EFLI	LIFE	You've got to love ____ to have _____
EECTERYM	CEMETERY	Setting for most of Act III
TIERDO	EDITOR	Mr. Webb's occupation
REGGEO	GEORGE	Rebecca's brother
EIAPXNPD	APPENDIX	Wally Webb's burst
HDTAE	DEATH	The end of one's life
OWNT	TOWN	Our _____
NECES	SCENE	Act division
RWIELD	WILDER	Author
TAC	ACT	Play division
OODRCT	DOCTOR	Mr. Gibbs is one

VOCABULARY RESOURCE MATERIALS

VOCABULARY WORD SEARCH - *Our Town*

All words in this list are associated with *Our Town* with an emphasis on the vocabulary words chosen for study in the text. The words are placed backwards, forward, diagonally, up and down. The included words are listed below.

```
P V S D R W G F R Z J V Y Z J T E M C S J H B J
L Y H G K R K L G Q S Y B L N Y W T X D V B N Y
H E L I O T R O P E B E R E A V E D E K U E L Y
C A G T X S M L B H T P C D P N E N G R R G F W
B H B A A M S H U A O I V N L T A N G R N T S T
M U W R C B M I C G T S Y D I E I L A I A A E G
P X R C U Y L I P S U T P E W V E B T F V X L N
D R N D X P L E U I N B C H I D O I F L A A E N
Q L O Y O I T J A E N N R R A S B R T S D L Q D
S G S S S C N L G U O G T I E T O W P N L R E H
C C F L C I K I Y C T N N S O N E E A A M H D Y
S N L F Z E L P N G O H I I T U R C F D S Y P L
N M Z H M I N B B C J L D E L A S T Z I N K F X
K N Z W D F K I T J L R D K T W S N U C R S V N
L N Q T N S G Z U E Q N T I H E O G E P C L B S
F W X P S R L L R M R S O F R B N C Y S J F T C
J F R G Y W Y T S M V N C C D A Z Z S Z S P F K
```

ABRUPTLY	BURGLE	GOSSIPING	PROVINCES
AFFRONTED	CONCEITED	HELIOTROPE	SCANDAL
ANGUISHED	CONTRIVING	INJUSTICE	SCOWLING
BARREN	CRESTFALLEN	LEGACY	SILICATE
BEREAVED	DILIGENT	LUGUBRIOUSNESS	TABLEAU
BITINGLY	ETERNAL	PHOSPHATE	TRELLISES
BURDOCK	EXASPERATION	PROSCENIUM	WEANED

VOCABULARY CROSSWORD - *Our Town*

VOCABULARY CROSSWORD CLUES - *Our Town*

ACROSS
2. Marked by persevering, painstaking effort
6. Choose the --- important day of your life; it will be important enough.
8. Gossipy choir member
13. What the ladies did at the wedding
14. Intentionally insulted
15. Baseball catcher's glove
16. Single
18. An incident that brings about disgrace or offends society
20. Structures used for supporting vines & creeping plants
21. Mr. Crowell
23. Small talk; chit-___
24. Agonized; tormented
26. George & Rebecca talk about it before going to sleep
27. Rebecca's last name
28. Affirmative answer to a proposal
29. Too
34. Slowly detached from something one is used to having
36. Observe; take note of
37. Oh, ---, you are too wonderful for anybody to realize you!
38. Empty; bare
39. Author
41. Howie delivered it
42. 9 baseball players make one
43. None; not any; zilch
44. Our ----
45. Steal
47. Detail often overlooked; red, blue, or green for example
50. Negative reply
51. Suffering the loss of a loved one
54. Stage area between curtain and orchestra
55. Marriage ceremony

DOWN
1. Mr. Gibbs is one
3. Having no particular interest or concern for
4. Violation of another's rights or of what is right
5. Feeling of impatient anger or annoyance
7. Act division
8. Craig; Mrs. Gibbs' nephew
9. Play division
10. Frowning in anger or disapproval
11. You've got to love --- to have ---
12. Areas situated away from the population center
17. Handed down from an ancestor
18. Compound containing silicon, oxygen and one or more metals
19. Not alive
22. A soda fountain drink with carbonated water & flavored syrup
25. Spreading rumors or talk of a personal or sensational nature
26. Stage ---; gives audience background info
30. Flowers native to Peru, having fragrant, purple flowers
31. Prickly, weed-like plant with purple flower
32. Planning with cleverness or ingenuity
33. His drinking problem is a scandal
35. Lasting forever
40. An interlude during a scene when all performers freeze momentarily
46. Act Two was about ---- and marriage
48. Something that is gone
49. Baseball ---; head covering
52. To become dead
53. Unusual

VOCABULARY CROSSWORD ANSWER KEY - *Our Town*

VOCABULARY WORKSHEET 1 - *Our Town*

___ 1. Spreading rumors or talk of a personal or sensational nature
    a. Scowling   b. Lugubriousness   c. Diligent   d. Gossiping

___ 2. Prickly, weed-like plant with purple flower
    a. Scowling   b. Burdock   c. Heliotrope   d. Phosphate

___ 3. Marked by persevering, painstaking effort
    a. Barren   b. Legacy   c. Diligent   d. Proscenium

___ 4. Steal
    a. Heliotrope   b. Burgle   c. Affronted   d. Tableau

___ 5. In a nasty way intending to hurt someone
    a. Burdock   b. Bitingly   c. Provinces   d. Trellises

___ 6. Structures used for supporting vines & creeping plants
    a. Diligent   b. Legacy   c. Trellises   d. Bereaved

___ 7. Empty; bare
    a. Burdock   b. Barren   c. Lugubriousness   d. Tableau

___ 8. Something handed down from an ancestor
    a. Scowling   b. Indifferent   c. Heliotrope   d. Legacy

___ 9. An incident that brings about disgrace or offends society
    a. Scandal   b. Trellises   c. Eternal   d. Affronted

___ 10. Suffering the loss of a loved one
    a. Phosphate   b. Contriving   c. Bereaved   d. Scowling

___ 11. An interlude during a scene when all performers freeze momentarily
    a. Injustice   b. Tableau   c. Crestfallen   d. Proscenium

___ 12. Intentionally insulted
    a. Burgle   b. Contriving   c. Trellises   d. Affronted

___ 13. Violation of another's rights or of what is right
    a. Diligent   b. Trellises   c. Proscenium   d. Injustice

___ 14. Compound containing silicon, oxygen and one or more metals
    a. Silicate   b. Lugubriousness   c. Legacy   d. Scandal

___ 15. Gloominess; ridiculously dismal
    a. Injustice   b. Lugubriousness   c. Phosphate   d. Scandal

___ 16. Dejected; dispirited or depressed
    a. Anguished   b. Crestfallen   c. Silicate   d. Diligent

___ 17. Planning with cleverness or ingenuity
    a. Proscenium   b. Trellises   c. Contriving   d. Diligent

___ 18. Having no particular interest or concern for
    a. Indifferent   b. Provinces   c. Eternal   d. Contriving

___ 19. Frowning in anger or disapproval
    a. Weaned   b. Gossiping   c. Crestfallen   d. Scowling

___ 20. Slowly detached from something one is used to having
    a. Scowling   b. Conceited   c. Bereaved   d. Weaned

VOCABULARY WORKSHEET 2 - *Our Town*

___ 1. PHOSPHATE   A. Lasting forever

___ 2. ABRUPTLY   B. Frowning in anger or disapproval

___ 3. SILICATE   C. Violation of another's rights or of what is right

___ 4. PROVINCES   D. An interlude during a scene when all performers freeze momentarily

___ 5. DILIGENT   E. Intentionally insulted

___ 6. INDIFFERENT   F. Dejected; Dispirited or depressed

___ 7. ETERNAL   G. Stage area between curtain and orchestra

___ 8. SCOWLING   H. Spreading rumors or talk of a personal or sensational nature

___ 9. TRELLISES   I. Vain; holding an unusually high opinion of oneself

___ 10. GOSSIPING   J. Compound containing silicon, oxygen and one or more metals

___ 11. PROSCENIUM   K. Marked by persevering, painstaking effort

___ 12. SCANDAL   L. In a short or brusque manner

___ 13. BURDOCK   M. Areas situated away from the population center

___ 14. TABLEAU   N. An incident that brings about disgrace or offends society

___ 15. HELIOTROPE   O. Flowers native to Peru, having fragrant, purple flowers

___ 16. AFFRONTED   P. A soda fountain drink with carbonated water & flavored syrup

___ 17. INJUSTICE   Q. Having no particular interest or concern for

___ 18. BURGLE   R. Prickly, weed-like plant with purple flower

___ 19. CONCEITED   S. Steal

___ 20. CRESTFALLEN   T. Structures used for supporting vines & creeping plants

KEY: VOCABULARY WORKSHEETS - *Our Town*

Worksheet 1	Worksheet 2
1. D	1. P
2. B	2. L
3. C	3. J
4. B	4. M
5. B	5. K
6. C	6. Q
7. B	7. A
8. D	8. B
9. A	9. T
10. C	10. H
11. B	11. G
12. D	12. N
13. D	13. R
14. A	14. D
15. B	15. O
16. B	16. E
17. C	17. C
18. A	18. S
19. D	19. I
20. D	20. F

VOCABULARY JUGGLE LETTER REVIEW GAME CLUES - *Our Town*

SCRAMBLED	WORD	CLUE
SSNGIGOPI	GOSSIPING	Spreading rumors or talk of a personal or sensational nature
ELTCLRFEANS	CRESTFALLEN	Dejected; dispirited or depressed
INIOCNGRVT	CONTRIVING	Planning with cleverness or ingenuity
INTEECODC	CONCEITED	Vain; holding an usually high opinion of oneself
LANEERT	ETERNAL	Lasting forever
ERNRBA	BARREN	Empty; bare
ENDEWA	WEANED	Slowly detached from something one is used to having
SLERISLET	TRELLISES	Structures used for supporting vines and creeping plants
REPOELTOHI	HELIOTROPE	Flowers native to Peru, having fragrant purple flowers
URTALBYP	ABRUPTLY	In a short or brusque manner
REIATOXANESP	EXASPERATION	Feeling of impatient anger or annoyance
ACEYGL	LEGACY	Something handed down from an ancestor
ERBLUG	BURGLE	Steal
BAEULTA	TABLEAU	An interlude during a scene when all performers freeze momentarily
DASALCN	SCANDAL	An incident that brings about disgrace or offends society
LBIYGINT	BITINGLY	In a nasty way intending to hurt someone
IUHSEGDNA	ANGUISHED	Agonized; tormented
SEPHTOPAH	PHOSPHATE	A soda fountain drink with carbonated water and flavored syrup
JEIITNCSU	INJUSTICE	Violation of another's rights or of what is right
GENLDTII	DILIGENT	Marked by persevering, painstaking effort
EOSNRUMPCI	PROSCENIUM	Stage area between curtain and orchestra
EIFTNFIERDN	INDIFFERENT	Having no particular interest or concern for
ILECISAT	SILICATE	Compound containing silicon, oxygen and one or more metals
ODRTFAENF	AFFRONTED	Intentionally insulted
COKBRUD	BURDOCK	Prickly, weed-like plant with purple flower
ERBVEEDA	BEREAVED	Suffering the loss of a loved one
CGLSONWI	SCOWLING	Frowning in anger or disapproval

www.ingramcontent.com/pod-product-compliance
Lightning Source LLC
Chambersburg PA
CBHW051418070526
44584CB00023B/3483